MW01490261

FALL 2019

SEP MATTHEW
OCT MARK
NOV JOHN
DEC ACTS

ontrack devotions

OnTrack Devotions: Fall 2019

Published by:
Pilgrimage
Boca Raton, FL
www.simplyapilgrim.com

For subscription information:

ontrackdevotions.com

Printed in the United States of America

Copyright © 2019 Pilgrimage

Author: Dwight E. Peterson
Executive Developer: Benjamin J. Wilhite
Editor: Kristin N. Jones

ISBN-13 978-0-9600241-1-7
10 9 8 7 6 5 4 3 2 1

Everyone is at a different place in their walk with God and in their Bible study skill. Because of that, OnTrack is designed to engage four progressive user **SKILL LEVELS**. This guide will help you identify your skill level and how to use OnTrack effectively.

IDENTIFY YOUR PERSONAL SKILL LEVEL

Be honest about your own personal level as you begin! Starting beyond your actual level can lead to unnecessary frustration and discouragement. Some level of frustration is good when learning a skill, but too much may tempt you to give up. Pay particular attention to the approach each user should take based on their current **SKILL LEVEL.**

Level 1: You have spent little or no time in personal Bible study and you have limited knowledge of the Bible. **FOCUS: Key Passage, Devotional Thought.**

Level 2: Most of your experience with the Bible is from church and/or at home. You have been taught from the Bible, but you have not consistently studied it on your own. **FOCUS: Extra Reading, Devotional Thought, answer at least the first two Daily Questions if you can.**

Level 3: You have a bit of experience reading the Bible on your own. Maybe it hasn't always been consistent or you are newer at it, but you are getting comfortable with it. **FOCUS: Extra Reading, Devotional Thought, answer all four Daily Questions.**

Level 4: You have a lot of experience in Bible study and you consistently see solid applications. **Focus: Extra Reading, Devotional Thought, all Daily Questions, and try creating your own questions.**

Every once in awhile, review your current skill level to check whether you should bump it up. You can do this on your own, with an accountability partner, or with a spiritual mentor. Aim to grow!

HOW TO USE ONTRACK

This tool is designed to help you grow your personal Bible study skill as a key part of developing a regular personal conversation with God. You will learn to dig into the text with good questions that lead to understanding and personal life change. To get the most out of OnTrack, follow the progression below:

PRAY. Ask the Holy Spirit to show you exactly what He wants you to see and understand from the Word. If you are in Christ, the Holy Spirit is in you and one of His jobs is to illuminate Scripture for you. He was the person of the Godhead directly engaged in the inspiration of the Word and He knows exactly what He meant when He wrote it.

READ THE WORD. Always start with reading the passage first before reading the devotional thought or any other tools you use to help understand Scripture.

What God has to say is always more important than what anyone else has to say about what God has to say.

READ THE DEVOTIONAL THOUGHT. The purpose of this text is to frame your thinking and to spur good questions, not to tie the passage up with a neat tidy bow.

ANSWER THE QUESTIONS. Some days, the author provides specific questions for you to answer that will help you dig into the text a bit. Other days, you'll see the generic Observation, Interpretation, Application, and Implementation questions. These are days designed to stretch you in the process of creating your own good questions.

ENGAGE OTHERS. One of the key benefits of a tool like OnTrack is that others in your world are working through the same Bible passages every day and engaging the same questions. This provides accountability for you; but more than that, it gives you an opportunity to compare notes and learn with each other. Often, you will see things they did not and vice versa. Bible study can be a team sport! It will help deepen your understanding of Scripture and your relationships.

GET ORIENTED
The following is a quick orientation to a typical OTD day. Use the sample devotional day image on the opposite page for reference.

1. **Header Bar:** It gives you the day of the week, the date, the theme, and the key passage for the day. Read the passage in your Bible BEFORE jumping to the next step!
2. **Extra Reading:** This is the complete text for the day. The key passage from the header bar will be in there, but this covers the context of the passage. If you are ready to bite off the whole chunk of Scripture, go for it!
3. **Devotional Thought:** The daily thought is designed to frame your thinking process AFTER you read the verses and BEFORE you answer the questions. It will encourage you to chew on the verses and ponder what God is telling you through His Word. The thought models for you the method of Bible study you are learning for yourself.
4. **Questions:** Each day will have four questions that help you personally work through the process of identifying what God is saying in His Word, then connecting it to your own life. Each question builds on the one before it.

A FINAL NOTE
Be patient and consistent. It's a process. Go at a comfortable pace. Ask God to grow your skill and to give you the discipline to keep at it. It will take time, but if you stick with it, you will be able to study God's Word for yourself.

1 TIMOTHY 1:12-17

SO THAT

1

SAY WHAT?

Observation: What do I see?

SO WHAT?

Interpretation: What does it mean?

4

NOW WHAT?

Application: How does it apply to me?

THEN WHAT?

Implementation: What do I do?

How do you feel when you think about what it means to be saved? Too often, people seem to be apathetic about their salvation, especially those saved as children. It is almost as if it all seems to be fairly routine to them. What they sometimes miss is the incredible reality of what happened and why it happened. Paul had never gotten over the fact that Jesus Christ had saved him. He stressed that, in spite of his behavior and past, God had, by His grace, changed his life. In verse 16, he explained why God had saved him. It was so his life would be an example to others of what Jesus Christ could do. Even though he was once a "violent man," he was changed by Christ. His own salvation gave hope to other violent men. What difference has believing in Jesus Christ made in your life? How is your life different from those who do not know Christ? Is there someone you know who needs to see and hear the ways in which Christ changed your life? Your life is an example of what God can do. Can the unsaved see it? Circle the words "so that in me" in your Bible to remind you of your mission. Then ask God to use you.

3

EXTRA READING
1 TIMOTHY 1

2

AGAIN I TELL YOU, IT IS EASIER FOR A CAMEL TO GO THROUGH THE EYE OF A NEEDLE THAN FOR A RICH PERSON TO ENTER THE KINGDOM OF GOD."

MATTHEW 19:24 (ESV)

ontrackdevotions.com

 @ontrackdevos

f facebook.com/ontrackdevos

SEPTEMBER
2019
MATTHEW

MONTHLY PRAYER SHEET

"...The prayer of a righteous man is powerful and effective." James 5:16

Reach out...	How I will do it...	How it went...

Other requests...	Answered	How it was answered...

Name: Katelynn

This sheet is designed to help you make personal commitments each month that will help you grow in your walk with God. Fill it out by determining
1. What will push you
2. What you think you can achieve

If you need help filling out your commitments, seek out someone you trust who can help you. Share your commitments with those who will help keep you accountable to your personal commitment.

my commitment is:

Personal Devotions:
How did I do with my commitment last month?_____
I will commit to read the OnTrack Bible passage and devotional thought _____ day(s) each week this month.

Church Attendance: *to do this for me!*
How did I do last month with my attendance? _____
I will attend Youth/Growth Group_____ time(s) this month.
I will attend the Sunday AM service_____ time(s) this month.
I will attend the Sunday PM service_____ time(s) this month.
I will attend_____ time(s) this month.
I will attend_____ time(s) this month.

Scripture Memory:
How did I do with Scripture memory last month? _____
I will memorize_____ key verse(s) from the daily OnTrack Devotions this month.

Outreach:
How did I do last month with sharing Christ? _____
I will share Christ with _____ person/people this month.
I will serve my local church this month by _____
_____

Other Activities:
List any other opportunities such as events, prayer group, etc., that you will participate in this month._____
_____

As you read through the genealogy of Christ, what thoughts go through your mind? As you look at His genealogy what do you notice about the people who are listed? Do they seem to be great people or common people or maybe even despicable people? We live in a society that tries to blame the negative characteristics of individuals on something other than themselves. If someone is a drug addict, a poor father, a failing student, etc., we try to determine what circumstance in their life made them like that. One explanation often suggested is their background. As a result, people often look at their background and think their destiny is determined by who their parents are, where they grew up, etc. We can learn from today's reading that, although Christ's genealogy listed many wicked people, that did not determine the kind of person Christ was. You may not have a background that would appear to set you up for greatness, but it does not guarantee failure either. God designed your background to best prepare you for His plan. God uses your history to help, not limit you. Are you allowing it to?

SAY WHAT?

What in a person's background could cause them to wonder if God can use them?

Drugs, Sex, Abuse

SO WHAT?

What reasons could God have for giving someone a background that is not as desirable as others?

Being able to connect with others

NOW WHAT?

How can you avoid allowing your own or someone else's background to become an obstacle to spiritual growth?

Focus on them nothing else

THEN WHAT?

In light of this passage, what personal commitment can you make?

Try looking at the person not the history.

EXTRA READING
MATTHEW 1

SAY WHAT?
Observation: What do I see?

Joseph following God

SO WHAT?
Interpretation: What does it mean?

All the prophecies were fufilled

NOW WHAT?
Application: How does it apply to me?

That Jesus really was the Son of God

THEN WHAT?
Implementation: What do I do?

Continue loving God

Whenever a phrase is repeated in a passage, it is generally a sign that it is there for a reason. There is a phrase used many times in today's reading that falls into this category. Did you notice it? It is the phrase "was fulfilled." One of the reasons the book of Matthew was written was to show the nation of Israel that Jesus Christ was the Messiah. Matthew needed to demonstrate that Jesus had a rightful claim to the throne, and that He was the fulfillment of the Old Testament prophecies. Throughout this book the phrase "was fulfilled" is used to describe who Jesus Christ truly was. Every decision that Joseph and Mary made in today's reading is a fulfillment of prophecy about the Messiah made thousands of years before. How could the Jews have missed what is so obvious to us? As you read this book, count the number of times you read the phrase, "was fulfilled" or "to fulfill." Hopefully, as the number increases, you will have even greater confidence that Jesus Christ was the Messiah sent from God to take away our sin. May that confidence cause you to tell others who Jesus Christ is! The people in our world need know.

EXTRA READING
MATTHEW 2

ontrackdevotions.com

In order to do the will of God, what did John the Baptist have to give up? What did it cost him to follow Christ and be His disciple? What might it cost for you to follow Christ? In some cases, like John's, it may require a lot. Becoming a disciple may involve having to live in a place that is not as comfortable as you would like, eating food that you may not like or dressing in a way that is different, like John the Baptist. If following Christ meant these kinds of changes for you, would you still be a disciple? It may mean leaving your business and choosing a different career, like Peter and Andrew did. If being a disciple meant pursuing a different career than the one you are now interested in, would you still be a disciple of Christ? For John the Baptist, Andrew, and Peter, the choice was not a hard one. They wanted to follow Christ regardless of the cost involved. Why? Because they loved Him and He alone had what they were looking for. What are you willing to give up in order to fully follow Christ? Maybe a better question is, what is preventing you from following Christ with all you have and all you are? Are you willing to give it up?

SAY WHAT?
What cost was required of the 12 disciples?

SO WHAT?
What may the cost be in order to be a disciple of Christ today?

NOW WHAT?
What should you be willing to give up in order to be a disciple of Christ?

THEN WHAT?
What personal commitment can you make in light of this passage?

EXTRA READING
MATTHEW 3, 4

 ontrack devotions

 #ontrackdevos

SAY WHAT?
Observation: What do I see?

SO WHAT?
Interpretation: What does it mean?

NOW WHAT?
Application: How does it apply to me?

THEN WHAT?
Implementation: What do I do?

How did Jesus Christ change what the people of that day believed was true religion? If you look closely at the Beatitudes, you find He did not really change the definition, but rather made it more difficult to obey. At first glance, it appears as if Jesus was teaching that the law was wrong and He revised and corrected it. In actuality, He took what they accepted as law one step further. For example, He said that they had heard murder was wrong, but He told them that it is wrong to even become angry with your brother. They had heard it was wrong to commit adultery. He said that it is wrong to have lustful thoughts. Through this, He demonstrated that His expectation for godliness was greater than they thought. We often look at our external behavior and feel acceptable because we do not violate obvious Biblical standards. God would say that while that is good, there is more than the obvious to be concerned about. While Christ did not say that the heart issue was equal to the external action, He did say the heart issue was sin. We need to examine our hearts for the beginning signs of sin and deal with them. We must not be satisfied to simply avoid the external act.

EXTRA READING
MATTHEW 5

ontrackdevotions.com

How many times in this chapter did Matthew use the words "in secret?" Why did he emphasize that we should do these kinds of spiritual activities when no one can see what we are doing? One of the reasons was that the religious rulers made public their attempts at worship and were prideful when people noticed. He does not want us to follow that wrong example. A second reason is what it says about our motives. We can tell a lot about ourselves by comparing our behavior while people are watching to our behavior when they are not. If our motivation is to please people, we will usually do things so they will notice and reward or compliment us. If we do it in secret, when no one is watching or even knows about it, then our motivation is more likely about pleasing God. Christ wanted these people to be aware that they should seek to please God alone. Do your acts of worship reveal a motive that is concerned with pleasing God or pleasing people? When you pray, give, or fast, do it only to please God. Our love for God needs to be our motivation and focus. Is it yours?

SAY WHAT?

How can you tell whether the motive of your behavior is to please God or people?

SO WHAT?

In what areas do you struggle the most in seeking to please people more than God?

NOW WHAT?

What can you do to avoid seeking the attention of people instead of God?

THEN WHAT?

In light of this passage, what personal commitment can you make?

EXTRA READING

MATTHEW 6

ontrack devotions

#ontrackdevos

SAY WHAT?

How would you evaluate the standards you use in judging others?

SO WHAT?

When God uses that same standard in judging you, what will your judgment be like?

NOW WHAT?

What can you do to become a more gracious and forgiving person in judging others?

THEN WHAT?

What personal commitment can you make in light of this passage?

In today's reading, we find a verse with serious implications in the life of a believer. It is one that should have great impact on our attitude and response toward others. Did you notice it? Verse 2 tells us that we will be judged in the same way that we judge others. Also, Matthew tells us that we will be judged according to the same measure that we use in judging others. That means if we are highly critical and pick on everything in someone's life, then God will judge us the same way. What does that mean for you? We are often critical of others. We judge them as though they should be perfect. We tolerate very few mistakes. When they fail, we jump all over them. Think about what that means for you. Since God will judge you the same way that you judge your family members, how will you do? Since God will use the same measure that you use for judging teachers, pastors, and other authorities in your life, how are you going to do when it is time for God to judge you? This passage ought to motivate us to be kind, generous, tolerant and forgiving people. Use today's questions to help you get started. Judgment day is coming!

EXTRA READING
MATTHEW 7

ontrackdevotions.com

If you had been living in Jesus Christ's day, who would you have thought He was? If you had known about the events we read in this chapter, you would have had to believe He was God. Just think about it for a moment. First, we see that He commanded the wind and the waves, and they obeyed Him. Imagine that you were in the midst of a storm that was about to take your life, and Jesus stood up, spoke, and the sea got quiet. Second, demons were shouting from within two men, calling Jesus the Son of God, and then asking what He was going to do with them. It was obvious Jesus had power over them, and they knew a day was coming when He would torture them forever. They wanted to know if that day were here or if He would wait until the appointed time. If you were there when those two events took place, would you have believed? Doesn't it make you wonder how people missed that Jesus was God. Yet, people are still missing Him today. We see Him work in our lives and demonstrate His power, yet we miss who He is. Are you or someone you know like these people? What can you do about it?

SAY WHAT?
Observation: What do I see?

SO WHAT?
Interpretation: What does it mean?

NOW WHAT?
Application: How does it apply to me?

THEN WHAT?
Implementation: What do I do?

EXTRA READING
MATTHEW 8

ontrack devotions

#ontrackdevos

PROVERBS 4

The book of Proverbs was designed to help us in "attaining wisdom and discipline; in understanding words of insight; in acquiring a disciplined and prudent life, doing what is right and just and fair; in giving prudence to the simple, knowledge and discretion to the young." As you read through this chapter, write down the verses that are most significant to you in your present circumstances.

VERSE | WHAT TRUTH IT COMMUNICATES | HOW IT IMPACTS MY LIFE

What does today's reading reveal to us about Jesus Christ? If you ask people you meet today who Jesus Christ is, what answers might they give? A common answer is that He was a good teacher or a prophet. This chapter proves that He could not have been either of those. Today we read that Jesus healed a paralytic man and also forgave his sins. The teachers of the law heard this and believed that Jesus blasphemed by claiming to be God, who alone can forgive sins. The passage also tells us that Jesus knew they thought He was claiming to be God. A mere teacher or a prophet would, at this moment, attempt to correct their assumption. Jesus, however, told them that He said what He did to prove that He had the power to forgive sins and was God. He either had to be God or He intentionally deceived people. We must believe Jesus to be God or conclude that He was a dangerous man. He could not have been a teacher or prophet and conducted himself in this manner. We must let people know that Jesus Christ is God and He came to forgive sin. It is our responsibility to let them know.

SAY WHAT?
Observation: What do I see?

SO WHAT?
Interpretation: What does it mean?

NOW WHAT?
Application: How does it apply to me?

THEN WHAT?
Implementation: What do I do?

EXTRA READING
MATTHEW 9

ontrack devotions

#ontrackdevos

SAY WHAT?

How can you tell what someone's motivation is for ministry?

SO WHAT?

What other motives might someone have in using their gifts, besides glorifying God and helping others?

NOW WHAT?

How could someone safeguard themselves from using their gifts for personal gain?

THEN WHAT?

What personal commitment can you make in light of today's passage?

Why did Jesus give the instructions found in verses 7-10 of today's reading? While there could be several reasons, one may be to demonstrate the proper motivation for ministry. Since the disciples had received amazing power, they could have easily been tempted to use that power for personal gain. If someone wanted to be healed, all he would have had to do would be to pay the disciples a sum of money. Who, in the midst of a life threatening illness, would not pay great sums of money to be healed? What would you pay to have a your mother, father or sibling raised from the dead? Jesus also told them not to take money or extra clothes. He wanted them to be dependent on Him to provide for their needs and be motivated only by love and a sincere desire to meet the needs of people. Money should not ever be a condition for which someone receives or gives ministry from God. We need people to use their gifts freely to help others and not for personal gain. If God is using you in the lives of people, make sure you do it to please Him, not yourself!

EXTRA READING
MATTHEW 10

What words did Christ use in today's reading to describe the Christian life? Would you use those same words? Would you use the word "easy" when describing your walk with God? When asked about the kinds of burdens that Christians must carry, would you describe them as "light?" How different our perspective on the Christian life is compared to what Jesus says in this chapter. He admonished us to come to Him if we were weary and burdened. Why? Because His yoke is easy and His burden is light. Much too often, we act as if being a Christian is so hard or difficult. We walk around dejected, wondering if we can make it through another day. We ask for prayer as if our lives are miserable and we might not get through this problem. But Jesus says His yoke is easy and His burden is light. The world should see Christians as people who view life as a great adventure, who trust God and see everything from His hand. We need to pick our chins up and stop wallowing in despair. His yoke is easy and His burden is light! So act like it! The world will notice if you do. Use today's questions to help you get started.

SAY WHAT?

What difficult circumstances have you faced that you view as burdens?

SO WHAT?

What has God said in His Word about difficulties like the ones listed above?

NOW WHAT?

What is God accomplishing or could He accomplish in your life through those burdens?

THEN WHAT?

In light of what this passage teaches, what personal commitment can you make?

EXTRA READING
MATTHEW 11

#ontrackdevos

SAY WHAT?
Observation: What do I see?

SO WHAT?
Interpretation: What does it mean?

NOW WHAT?
Application: How does it apply to me?

THEN WHAT?
Implementation: What do I do?

Why was it important for Jesus to identify Himself as being the "Lord of the Sabbath?" When you understand what that statement means, you understand why using it was so significant. In this passage, the Pharisees accused Jesus and His disciples of violating what the Old Testament Law said about the Sabbath. Anyone who violated the Sabbath was guilty of breaking the law. Were Jesus and the disciples guilty of breaking the law? If so, then Jesus could not be the Messiah as He claimed. Jesus told the Pharisees that He could do what He chose to on the Sabbath because He was "Lord of the Sabbath." By this statement, He implied that because He is God and the law was created by Him, it can be changed by Him, and responded to by Him however He chooses. This statement was a clear claim of deity by Jesus. He essentially said, "I did what I did and am saying what I am now saying because I am God!" It is another clear example in which Jesus Himself claimed to be God and not just a teacher or a prophet. God's Word is clear about who Jesus said He was. We must be convinced ourselves that Jesus is God, and let others know. Are you?

EXTRA READING
MATTHEW 12

ontrackdevotions.com

Most know there needs to be fruit in our lives as evidence of our salvation, but how much fruit do you need to see to be confident of your salvation? The answer found in today's reading should encourage us. In this parable, Jesus explains the different responses to the Gospel. In the third response, He states that this person is not saved because he has no fruit. In verse 23, He tells us that one who is truly saved, hears the Word and it produces a crop. How big a crop? According to the passage, it depends on the person. In some cases, it is 100 fold. In others, it is 60 or 30 fold. The point is not the amount of fruit, but that there is some fruit. It is easy to compare the fruit in your life to others and base the evidence of your salvation on that comparison. It will become discouraging if you continue to evaluate your salvation that way. What you need to ask yourself is whether you see any fruit. The amount can vary between people, but we should all see fruit. Use today's questions to help you examine your life and measure the progress or fruit in your walk with God. It could expose a problem. If it does, find someone who can help you.

SAY WHAT?

In what areas of your life have you seen fruit over the past year?

SO WHAT?

In what areas do you desire to see greater fruit?

NOW WHAT?

How can you ensure that you will continue to have greater fruit?

THEN WHAT?

What personal commitment can you make in light of this passage?

EXTRA READING
MATTHEW 13

ontrack devotions

#ontrackdevos

SAY WHAT?
Observation: What do I see?

SO WHAT?
Interpretation: What does it mean?

NOW WHAT?
Application: How does it apply to me?

THEN WHAT?
Implementation: What do I do?

What can we learn from this passage about our response when someone we love dies. Is it okay to cry and feel pain? We can learn a lot from the example of Jesus Christ's life in today's reading. In this chapter, we read the details surrounding the death of John the Baptist. Jesus, who was close to John, heard about it and the Scriptures tells us that "He withdrew privately to a solitary place." He was likely upset by the news and wanted to be alone. He left his companions to think and pray by Himself. But He didn't stay there. He soon got up and went back to His ministry and fulfilling God's purpose for His life. There are times when we are pained by the loss of someone we love and care deeply about. We may need to take some time to be alone, to privately work things through, but we must then pick ourselves up and get back to living our lives. Is there pain in your life that you are allowing to keep you from living the life God has called you to? Spending time to grieve is proper and necessary, and may take longer for some than others, but maybe it's time to get back to living. Could it be that time for you? What steps do you need to take?

EXTRA READING
MATTHEW 14

The book of Proverbs was designed to help us in "attaining wisdom and discipline; in understanding words of insight; in acquiring a disciplined and prudent life, doing what is right and just and fair; in giving prudence to the simple, knowledge and discretion to the young." As you read through this chapter, write down the verses that are most significant to you in your present circumstances.

VERSE	WHAT TRUTH IT COMMUNICATES	HOW IT IMPACTS MY LIFE

SAY WHAT?

In what areas of life is it difficult to have faith?

SO WHAT?

Why is it so hard to trust God in those areas?

NOW WHAT?

How can you begin to develop "great faith?"

THEN WHAT?

In light of this passage, what personal commitment can you make?

What does the story of the Canaanite woman teach us regarding faith? First, we learn that anyone who has true faith can come to God and He will respond to them. Although she was not a Jew, Jesus responded to her need and healed her daughter. Second, we find the characteristics of "great" faith. We learn that it is repentant faith. This faith realizes that God alone can meet your need. It is directed to the right source. True faith is trusting in Christ alone. It is persistent, knowing that God is in control and He can be trusted. It doesn't give up even when it appears God is not listening or does not care. Great faith keeps on trusting God and seeking Him. It is also humble. This woman knew she was sinful and unworthy of any response from Christ. She asked only for crumbs that might fall from the table. What is God's response to such faith? He met her need and told her she had great faith! What kind of faith do you have? Do you have "weak" faith like Peter in chapter 14 or "great" faith like this woman? Do you seek God in every area of your life? Do you have a humble spirit when you come to Him? Do you trust even when it looks bleak?

EXTRA READING

MATTHEW 15

What is the rock that Christ mentioned in verse 18 of today's reading? Some believe that the rock was Peter, concluding that Christ was stating that He will build His church upon Peter. In fact, the Catholic church bases much of its theology on this view. But a close examination of the text reveals something much more exciting. Christ had just asked His disciples who they think He is. Peter said that he believed Jesus was the Christ. This answer thrilled Jesus, not because Peter gave the right answer, but because the answer came from God. Peter's answer indicated that God had revealed truth to him. The rock to which Christ was referring was God revealing His truth to man. The pronoun refers not to Peter, but to Peter having information revealed to him from God. Christ builds His church on God's truth given to us through the Holy Spirit. Another thrilling truth found here is that the gates of hell can't keep God from revealing His truth to us. Satan cannot prevent the church from being built as a result of that truth. God wants to reveal Himself to you. Are you open to what God is saying? Do you take time each day to listen?

SAY WHAT?
Observation: What do I see?

SO WHAT?
Interpretation: What does it mean?

NOW WHAT?
Application: How does it apply to me?

THEN WHAT?
Implementation: What do I do?

EXTRA READING
MATTHEW 16

ontrack devotions

SAY WHAT?

What situations have you faced that seemed impossible to handle, yet God accomplished something great in your life?

SO WHAT?

When have you been surprised by what God has done on your behalf?

NOW WHAT?

What can you do to be less like the disciples and more trusting of God?

THEN WHAT?

In light of this passage, what personal commitment can you make?

How many times did Jesus tell the disciples in today's reading that He was going to rise from the dead? Number them in your Bible. It is astounding, after reading this section of Scripture, to realize how clearly Christ had explained to the disciples what was going to happen to Him in the future. How did they miss it? Why is it that when He died on the cross they were so fearful and scattered? Why were they so surprised when He rose again? Well, before we get too critical of them, remember how similar we are. Christ clearly tells us in His Word that everything that happens in my life is for my good and that He will always accomplish something wonderful through it. Yet, how often do you panic or grow anxious when something negative happens? He clearly promised that He will always meet our needs, yet we act so surprised when He does. We, like the disciples, need to learn to be more trusting of what God has clearly stated. In what area of your life do you struggle with doubt? Do you live in confidence of His promises? Have you been shocked by God's provision in your life? What can you do to change and become more trusting?

EXTRA READING

MATTHEW 17

In today's reading, we find the most commonly used passage to guide us in handling conflicts. In Christ's instruction, there is an important phrase that we often forget. It is found in verse 15. It is the phrase, "just between the two of you." If we believe someone has done something wrong, we are to approach them about it, keeping the matter between the two of us. It should be a private situation. While we may ask for help or advice from our parents or pastor on how we ought to handle it, we are not permitted to talk to friends, informing them of the situation or how we are going to resolve it. Bringing it up in conversations with others is wrong. Jesus' instruction is clear that we are to go talk to the person involved. We are only to involve others when we are unable to resolve it between the two of us. Are there conflicts or problems between you and someone else that you have discussed with others, but have not gone to the person directly? Determine today to handle conflicts in a Biblical way. Violating Scripture is never a means to solve conflict.

SAY WHAT?
Observation: What do I see?

SO WHAT?
Interpretation: What does it mean?

NOW WHAT?
Application: How does it apply to me?

THEN WHAT?
Implementation: What do I do?

EXTRA READING
MATTHEW 18

ontrack devotions

#ontrackdevos

SAY WHAT?
Observation: What do I see?

SO WHAT?
Interpretation: What does it mean?

NOW WHAT?
Application: How does it apply to me?

THEN WHAT?
Implementation: What do I do?

What point was Jesus trying to make to the young rich man in today's reading? The point is one that each of us needs to understand and readily share with others. This passage tells us that the rich man asked Jesus what to do in order to be saved. At first, it appears that Jesus told him that he could earn his way to Heaven by obeying the law. Then, it seems as if Christ told him to sell all he had to be able to gain eternal life. Was Jesus in fact saying this? Christ knew this man's heart and in fact was attempting to demonstrate that while he claimed to be ready to be saved, he was in reality unwilling to give up all he had to follow Christ. He was only interested in "adding" Christ to his life. This passage illustrates that we cannot get to Heaven by simply believing the right truth or by obeying the commandments of Scripture. To be saved one must come to God, humbly admitting he's a sinner, seeking His forgiveness, and being willing to sacrifice all for Him. The rich man did not get saved because he was unwilling to give up his wealth. Is there something you won't give up for Christ? Simply "adding" Christ to you life is not enough.

EXTRA READING
MATTHEW 19

As you read today's passage, which of the workers in the vineyard did you identify with? Did you rejoice with those that got a day's pay for only working one hour? Or did you think the people who worked all day should get more than those who only worked an hour? Jesus uses this story to illustrate another important principle. People come to Christ from all different backgrounds. Some are saved as children and walk with God from that day. Others come to Christ after years of rebellion and sin. The response? God welcomes them equally, and gives to both the same forgiveness. Some Christians view that as unfair. They feel that they are entitled to more because they have walked in obedience for many years. Some even become upset when someone in the church has sinned and God seems to graciously forgive. They would like to see more suffering for their sin. But God gives His love and forgiveness to all equally. We need to rejoice in God's goodness to all people and not be jealous of what He gives to others. We have already gotten more than we deserve, and are not facing the punishment due us!

SAY WHAT?

In what way do people today demonstrate the attitudes of this section?

SO WHAT?

How do those attitudes surface in your life?

NOW WHAT?

How can you guard yourself from these kinds of attitudes?

THEN WHAT?

What personal commitment can you make in light of today's reading?

EXTRA READING
MATTHEW 20

#ontrackdevos

PROVERBS 6

The book of Proverbs was designed to help us in "attaining wisdom and discipline; in understanding words of insight; in acquiring a disciplined and prudent life, doing what is right and just and fair; in giving prudence to the simple, knowledge and discretion to the young." As you read through this chapter, write down the verses that are most significant to you in your present circumstances.

VERSE | WHAT TRUTH IT COMMUNICATES | HOW IT IMPACTS MY LIFE

How did the money changers in today's reading make the temple into a den of robbers? Does this passage teach that there should be no selling of anything at church? The temple was supposed to be a place where people could come to worship God. When they came, they could feel secure and protected. The temple was supposed to be a place in which they did not have to worry about being taken advantage of or used. All they needed to focus on was worshiping God in total freedom. Instead, the temple had become the opposite of what God intended it to be. God's people entered and met those who were trying to take advantage of them. They had to fight their way through the sales pitch of the merchants to be able to worship. They faced people who were using them and the temple as a place to get rich. Jesus saw this and hated it. He cleared the temple to restore it for its purpose. How would Jesus feel today if He walked into your church? Is it a place where people feel secure, protected, and loved? Are people able to just come and worship? What can you do to help make it more a place of true worship?

SAY WHAT?
Observation: What do I see?

SO WHAT?
Interpretation: What does it mean?

NOW WHAT?
Application: How does it apply to me?

THEN WHAT?
Implementation: What do I do?

EXTRA READING
MATTHEW 21

ontrack devotions

#ontrackdevos

SAY WHAT?
Observation: What do I see?

SO WHAT?
Interpretation: What does it mean?

NOW WHAT?
Application: How does it apply to me?

THEN WHAT?
Implementation: What do I do?

What does the parable about the wedding banquet tell us about the kingdom of heaven? One clear message is that the Gospel invitation is open to everyone, but many do not respond to it. Everyone was told that the time for the wedding banquet had come. Everything was ready and in place, but some headed back to their fields or business. They were simply too involved in their own lives to think about God and His invitation. Some even mistreated the very people who had come to offer them salvation. So what is God's response to those who reject His invitation? To offer it to anyone and everyone. Jesus wanted everyone to have the opportunity to hear God's invitation. It is not only the rich, popular, kind, or friendly who can receive Christ. In fact, generally these people have no need for God. Their lives are going along quite smoothly. We need to let everyone know about God's invitation. Can you think of people in your world you have been unwilling to share God's invitation with? Is there someone at school or work that God has been prompting you about? Maybe you should start talking to them today.

EXTRA READING
MATTHEW 22

ontrackdevotions.com

In today's reading, we find three important principles about leadership. Did you notice them? They are found in Christ's condemnation of the Pharisees in verses 1-12. Jesus used what was wrong with their leadership to demonstrate what He expects of us. First, He said in verses 1-4, that a leader must always practice what he preaches. His words must match his actions. Second, He said that a leader must have the right motives. The Pharisees were motivated by pride. They wanted to be noticed and have the big title. A true leader cannot have a heart of pride. Third, Jesus said that a leader must be a servant. Unlike the Pharisees, they must be willing to serve others. They must not see themself as some big shot. They must humble themself and be willing to serve the needs of others. How well do you meet these qualifications? Do you practice what you preach? Do you look for attention and seek the praise of others? Do you always look to have people do things for you or are you willing to serve others? What needs to change in your life for you to meet these qualifications and become a leader in your world?

SAY WHAT?

In what areas do you struggle the most to practice what you preach? Why?

SO WHAT?

How can you tell what your motivation is for wanting a position of leadership?

NOW WHAT?

How can you tell if you are truly willing to serve others?

THEN WHAT?

In what area do you need to change to be the kind of leader described in this passage?

EXTRA READING
MATTHEW 23

 ontrack devotions

 #ontrackdevos

SAY WHAT?

Observation: What do I see?

SO WHAT?

Interpretation: What does it mean?

NOW WHAT?

Application: How does it apply to me?

THEN WHAT?

Implementation: What do I do?

Who was Jesus referring to as "this generation" in verse 34? If He were referring to the disciples, they would not pass away or die, until the kingdom came. They, of course, died and we could conclude that His statement was not true. If this statement was not true, then we could in turn wonder if other statements He made were also untrue. If He could be wrong about the time of His return, then He could be wrong about other matters. A closer look at the context, however, reveals Jesus was not referring to the disciples. He was referring to the generation that would see the signs already mentioned throughout the chapter. Verse 33 says that when you see these things you will know that the time is near. This generation, the one who sees these things, will then not pass away until all of it happens. To give us greater confidence in what he is saying, He told us that heaven and earth will pass away, but His Words will never pass away. How close are we to the end? According to Scripture, very close. Since God has never been wrong, we can be assured He will return just as He said. Are you ready? Are your friends?

EXTRA READING

MATTHEW 24

ontrackdevotions.com

Who are the "least of these" Jesus refers to in verse 45? Who are they in our world today? According to the passage, the "least of these" are people who are hungry, thirsty, strangers, and those lacking clothing. In other words it is those people in your world who have great needs. So often, we find it easy to reach out to the popular people or the people who are athletic or talented. We invite to our parties those who dress nicely and might be able to return the favor in the future. We do not reach out to those who are not well liked and have few friends. We act as if we do not want to be seen with those who are poor, those who are less fashionable, or who stand out for some negative reason. Jesus lets us know that whatever we do for these kinds of people we are, in fact, doing for Him. How successful are you in loving the "least of these" in your world? When is the last time you spent time with a "least of these" kind of person? Remember, whatever you do for them, God considers it something done for Him. What can you do today or this week for the "least of these" that you know in your world? Look around and get started today!

SAY WHAT?

Identify some people in your world who are considered " the least of these."

SO WHAT?

Why is it so hard for us to reach out to them?

NOW WHAT?

What can you do this week to begin to reach out to the "least of these" in your world?

THEN WHAT?

What personal commitment can you make in light of today's reading?

EXTRA READING
MATTHEW 25

ontrack
devotions

SAY WHAT?
Observation: What do I see?

SO WHAT?
Interpretation: What does it mean?

NOW WHAT?
Application: How does it apply to me?

THEN WHAT?
Implementation: What do I do?

Why did those who saw the woman break open the alabaster jar of perfume react negatively to what she did? The answer is in their comments found in verse 8, "Why this waste?" It is obvious from their reaction that they saw what she did as being a big waste. According to them, she should have used her perfume in a better way. At the very least she could have sold it and then given the money to the poor. But to waste it on the head of Jesus? While we consider their response to be wrong, it happens all the time today. If a person is talented in obvious ways, he or she is encouraged to aspire to big dreams and goals. Many view vocational ministry as being a waste of all that talent. If a bright and very talented young couple came forward in a service to share their decision to go to a foreign field to be missionaries, some tend to say, "what a waste." This woman demonstrated to us that God deserves the very best we have to offer. He gave us the specific abilities and talents necessary to have the most impact on our worlds for Him. Our abilities will never be wasted in vocational ministry. In fact, the waste may be using them elsewhere.

EXTRA READING
MATTHEW 26

What emotion did Judas have in today's reading? Is the emotion we are told he had the same as being repentant? The answer is no and the difference is important. In fact, the difference determines how God responds to us. In this passage, we see that Judas realized the consequences of his actions. Scripture tells us that he was seized with remorse. He felt bad about what he had done and tried to undo it. Remorse is feeling guilty or bad about something you have done and the consequences it has caused. Repentance is far more than that. Repentance is not only being sorry that I was caught doing wrong or sorry that my actions caused pain, but it is wanting to turn from them and never repeat them. It is changing my mind and my will about what I have done. I can feel really badly about something and not forsake it or seek forgiveness. I just feel bad it turned out wrong. While Judas felt remorse, he never repented of his sin and never sought the forgiveness of God. His guilt overwhelmed him, but it never led to repentance. Is there an area of your life in which you have remorse but not repentance? Don't let it destroy you like it did Judas.

SAY WHAT?
How can we tell if we have remorse or repentance over our sin?

SO WHAT?
In what areas of your life do you find it hard to have repentance and not just remorse?

NOW WHAT?
What can you do to make sure you have repentance over your sin and not just remorse?

THEN WHAT?
In light of this passage, what personal commitment can you make?

EXTRA READING
MATTHEW 27

ontrack devotions

#ontrackdevos

SAY WHAT?
Observation: What do I see?

SO WHAT?
Interpretation: What does it mean?

NOW WHAT?
Application: How does it apply to me?

THEN WHAT?
Implementation: What do I do?

Did you ever notice how hard some people work to avoid the truth? They try to ignore it, change it, or distort it, so they do not have to face it. They will do almost anything instead of just admitting something is the truth. An example of this is found in today's reading. Jesus Christ had risen from the dead. The guards saw it and they ran to tell the chief priests. One would assume that they would want to investigate and find the truth. Surely they would have checked the tomb for themselves. Instead, they came up with a plan to ignore it and make sure the truth never got out. The guards were paid to say that the disciples came to take the body away. Why would the guards accept payment to ignore the truth? After what they had seen, one would assume that nothing could make them deny what they knew to be truth. Often, we are guilty of the same thing. We hear something and know it is the truth, but we deny it and willfully ignore it. We may even get some of our friends to support us in the distortion of the truth. Could you being doing this? In what area of your life do you need to be honest and simply accept what you know to be true?

EXTRA READING
MATTHEW 28

For even the Son of Man did not come to be served, but to serve, and to give his life as a ransom for many.

--Mark 10:45 (NIV)

ontrackdevotions.com

 @ontrackdevos

 facebook.com/ontrackdevos

OCTOBER
2019
MARK

MONTHLY PRAYER SHEET

"...The prayer of a righteous man is powerful and effective." James 5:16

Reach out...	How I will do it...	How it went...

Other requests...	Answered	How it was answered...

Name: _____

This sheet is designed to help you make personal commitments each month that will help you grow in your walk with God. Fill it out by determining
    1. What will push you
    2. What you think you can achieve
If you need help filling out your commitments, seek out someone you trust who can help you. Share your commitments with those who will help keep you accountable to your personal commitment.

Personal Devotions:
How did I do with my commitment last month?_____
I will commit to read the OnTrack Bible passage and devotional thought _____day(s) each week this month.

Church Attendance:
How did I do last month with my attendance? _____
I will attend Youth/Growth Group_____ time(s) this month.
I will attend the Sunday AM service _____ time(s) this month.
I will attend the Sunday PM service _____ time(s) this month.
I will attend_____ time(s) this month.
I will attend_____ time(s) this month.

Scripture Memory:
How did I do with Scripture memory last month? _____
I will memorize _____ key verse(s) from the daily OnTrack Devotions this month.

Outreach:
How did I do last month with sharing Christ?_____
I will share Christ with _____ person/people this month.
I will serve my local church this month by _____
_____

Other Activities:
List any other opportunities such as events, prayer group, etc., that you will participate in this month. _____
_____

ontrack
devotions

#ontrackdevos

What does it take to be a fisher of men? What did it take for James and John? In today's passage, we read the details of James' and John's calling. In this account we learn something interesting. We discover that Jesus called them in front of their father and other hired hands and that they immediately decided to leave home to follow Him. In order for them to be fishers of men, they had to leave their father and walk away from a successful family business. A business that not only involved family but other partners and boats. Their fishing business must have been a large part of everyday discussions with their father and a source of security for their future. To follow Christ, in their case, meant to leave it all behind. Amazingly, they made a monumental decision on the spot, without any hesitation. They left it all behind to follow Christ, because the thought of becoming a fisher of men was more compelling than being a fisher of fish. Which option would be more exciting to you? Being a fisher of men or running the family business? Following Christ is the most exciting life one can have. Do you believe that enough to be willing to "leave" it all if that is what Jesus asked?

SAY WHAT?
Observation: What do I see?

SO WHAT?
Interpretation: What does it mean?

NOW WHAT?
Application: How does it apply to me?

THEN WHAT?
Implementation: What do I do?

EXTRA READING
MARK 1

ontrack devotions

#ontrackdevos

SAY WHAT?

What instructions have you been given that didn't seem to make sense at the time?

SO WHAT?

What did you later discover was the purpose?

NOW WHAT?

Are you struggling to obey an instruction that you know God wants you to obey?

THEN WHAT?

In light of this passage, what personal commitment can you make?

Have you ever had instructions given to you that made no sense at all? How did you respond to those instructions? In today's reading, we see an example of instructions that seem to make no sense. A man with leprosy came to Jesus to be healed. He had a disease that meant life as he knew it, was over. Not only was he going to die a terribly painful death, he would be an outcast forever. He would have to move out of his home and never have contact with people again. When someone came near him, he would have to call out, "unclean, unclean." No wonder he wanted to be healed. However, after he was healed, Jesus gave him surprising instructions. The leper was told to "say nothing to anyone" about what had happened, but show himself to the priest. He couldn't tell anyone. But, he went out and told his story anyway. As a result, Jesus' ministry was changed. He was no longer able to go into the towns but had to stay out in lonely places. When we find ourselves in similar situations, we need to trust what God tells us even when it seems to make no sense. We can't only obey instructions that we understand or agree with.

EXTRA READING
MARK 1

The Bible reveals to us that Jesus Christ was not just a prophet or a good teacher, He was in fact, God. Do you know where to direct a person who questions this truth? You could take him to this chapter. Jesus healed the paralytic and told him that his sins were forgiven. When the people heard this, they thought Jesus was claiming to be God because only God can forgive sins. Mark tells us that Jesus knew what they were thinking. If He were only a teacher or a prophet, He would have corrected their thoughts and told them that they had misunderstood what He had said. But He did not do that. In fact, He explained to them that He forgave the paralytic's sins so that they would "know" He was God. That was the whole point of His miracle. Jesus claimed, on a number of occasions, to be God. He knew what He was doing and what people thought. If He wasn't God He would have been a false prophet intentionally leading people astray. How do you respond to the fact that Jesus Christ is God? Who in your world needs to know who He is and what He has done for them? Will you be the one who will tell them?

SAY WHAT?
Observation: What do I see?

SO WHAT?
Interpretation: What does it mean?

NOW WHAT?
Application: How does it apply to me?

THEN WHAT?
Implementation: What do I do?

EXTRA READING
MARK 2

ontrack devotions

SAY WHAT?

How can you tell if the Gospel has priority in your life?

SO WHAT?

Why is it so easy for us to allow other things to become a priority over the Gospel?

NOW WHAT?

What needs to change in your life so the Gospel has greater priority?

THEN WHAT?

In light of this passage, what personal commitment can you make?

If you were to list the top three activities that Jesus and His disciples performed, what would they be? Would you put healing or casting out demons at the top of the list? Where would you put performing miracles? The item that occupied most of their time and was the number one priority might not even end up on some of our lists. It might surprise some that preaching and teaching were the most significant activities of their daily lives. We learn in verse 15 that Jesus first sent the disciples out to preach. It was their primary responsibility. We often think they were sent to heal the sick and cast out demons. While they did those things, their main concern, was to communicate the gospel message to those who would listen. Jesus Himself set that as His priority. In fact, one reason He often told people He healed not to tell others was so that He could continue preaching and avoid being swarmed by the many who wanted physical healing. If communicating the Gospel was the priority while Jesus was on the earth, how important should it be for us today? Is it your priority? Use today's questions to help you think through the priorities of your life and what needs to change.

EXTRA READING

MARK 3

Have you ever wanted to be a part of another family? You observe how much they love each other and wish you could be one of them. As you watch this family, you realize that they are committed to each other and you want that for yourself. In these verses we discover that we can be a part of the greatest family there is--the family of God. In verse 31, we read that Jesus' family stood outside waiting, after sending someone to get Him. Jesus responded to their arrival by looking at those seated there and telling them they could be a part of His family if they would do the will of His Father. This same truth applies to us also. If we do His will, we "are" His brothers and sisters. How incredible! We become a member of a family like no other. God is our Father, and we can go to Him as His child with anything. He cares for us because we are literally His children. Other believers from around the world become our brothers and sisters. We have a bond the world knows nothing about. How should you respond to such incredible truth? Will it impact your behavior today? Do you know of someone who would love to be part of the family of God? Will you find a way to tell him?

SAY WHAT?
Observation: What do I see?

SO WHAT?
Interpretation: What does it mean?

NOW WHAT?
Application: How does it apply to me?

THEN WHAT?
Implementation: What do I do?

EXTRA READING
MARK 3

ontrack devotions

#ontrackdevos

PROVERBS 7

The book of Proverbs was designed to help us in "attaining wisdom and discipline; in understanding words of insight; in acquiring a disciplined and prudent life, doing what is right and just and fair; in giving prudence to the simple, knowledge and discretion to the young." As you read through this chapter, write down the verses that are most significant to you in your present circumstances.

VERSE | WHAT TRUTH IT COMMUNICATES | HOW IT IMPACTS MY LIFE

How do we come to be able to understand spiritual truth? Why do some people seem to get it while others just become confused? The answer is found in today's reading, and it should be an encouragement to you. Jesus taught the crowd about the kingdom of God. He did so by using a parable. Later, when He was alone with His disciples, they asked Him to explain the parable. In His answer, we discover an important principle. Jesus told them in verse 11 that the truth "has been given to them." God planted it in their hearts. It did not come from superior intellect, but from God. Jesus revealed that understanding spiritual truth is a gift from God. While it is true that we need to work hard to learn skills that will enable us to better understand what the Bible says, it is God who gives us the understanding. Therefore, we must walk closely with Him so that we can receive understanding from Him. If we are not walking with Him, we deprive ourselves of spiritual understanding. Underline verse 11 to remind you of the source of our spiritual understanding and the need to walk with God. What an awesome privilege.

SAY WHAT?

What spiritual truths has God revealed to you recently?

SO WHAT?

How can you take advantage of the opportunities God gives to teach you truth?

NOW WHAT?

In what ways do you hinder God's revelation of spiritual truth in your life?

THEN WHAT?

In light of this passage, what personal commitment can you make?

EXTRA READING
MARK 4

ontrack devotions

#ontrackdevos

SAY WHAT?
Observation: What do I see?

SO WHAT?
Interpretation: What does it mean?

NOW WHAT?
Application: How does it apply to me?

THEN WHAT?
Implementation: What do I do?

Why is it that some people seem to have more ability to comprehend spiritual truth than others? Today's reading gives us an answer. Jesus followed up His discussion from yesterday's reading with the illustration of a lamp. He said that you do not take a lamp and put it in a place where it's light isn't seen. Why? It's light is meant to shine and not be hidden. In the same way, we are to take the light that God gives us, our spiritual understanding, and shine it, not keep it to ourselves or hide it. Jesus said that when God gives us spiritual understanding, we need to share it with others both verbally and by the way we live. If we use what we have been given as light, then He will give us more understanding. If we do not and keep it inside or not allow it to impact the way we live, even the understanding we have will be taken away. Have you discovered a truth about God recently that you could share with someone? Is what you are learning impacting the way you live? How are you going to let it shine? Spiritual truth was never meant to be hidden but to be acted upon and shared. Those who hide truth are those who will die spiritually.

EXTRA READING
MARK 4

ontrackdevotions.com

If you saw a man's life totally changed, what would your response be? Would it be fear? As we read the account in today's passage, we see that the townspeople responded to the demon possessed man's miracle with that emotion. This man had lived a life of misery for years. In fact, the passage says that night and day he would cry out in his pain. How chilling those sounds must have been. It must have been frightening to see a man so bound by Satan. Then one day, Jesus came along and the man's life radically changed. When the people saw him, they were afraid. What could they have feared? They weren't afraid because the pigs died. They didn't know about that until after they had seen that the man was changed. Why didn't they respond with joy or seek their own change? Could it be because of sin in their own lives. A stranger who could free a demon-possessed man could surely see into their hearts. Often seeing Jesus for who He is causes us to see ourselves for who we are. This can cause us to run in fear and not approach Him with humility and repentance. Do not allow your fear to cause you to miss an opportunity for God to change your life.

SAY WHAT?
Observation: What do I see?

SO WHAT?
Interpretation: What does it mean?

NOW WHAT?
Application: How does it apply to me?

THEN WHAT?
Implementation: What do I do?

EXTRA READING
MARK 5

ontrack devotions

#ontrackdevos

MARK 5:21-43

SAY WHAT?
Is there a hopeless circumstance in your life right now?

SO WHAT?
What are you afraid will happen?

NOW WHAT?
How can today's reading encourage you?

THEN WHAT?
In light of this passage, what personal commitment can you make?

Have you ever faced a situation that seemed hopeless? You prayed and asked God to move on your behalf, and it seems as though He has done nothing. You keep praying but before God responds, it is too late. If so, you must have identified with the synagogue ruler in today's reading. He risked a great deal by coming to Jesus in the first place. His situation was desperate, and his only concern was that his daughter be healed. He knew Jesus could heal her, but she died before He responded. Jairus was told that it was too late, and he should leave the teacher alone. Jesus ignored what was said and turned to him with these words, "Don't be afraid, just believe." It is never too late for God. The ruler, his heart gripped with fear and despair, was told by Jesus to "just believe." That man went with Jesus into his home while those around laughed. As a result of his belief, the man's daughter was healed. Are you facing a hopeless circumstance in your life? Ready to give up? Like Jairus, don't fear, just believe. Underline the words, "Don't be afraid, just believe," in your Bible to remind you that God is still in control and able to respond to your needs.

EXTRA READING
MARK 5

How would those who dislike you describe you to others? What words would they use? Would they use words similar to those Herod used to describe John the Baptist? Even though Herod disliked him, he knew that John was a righteous and holy man. Herod did not like John because John confronted him with his sin. Herod had married his brother's wife, Herodias. John knew it was sin and was not afraid to tell Herod so. As a result, both Herod and his wife were angry with him. John was in prison because Herodias pressured Herod into having him arrested. While in prison, Herod sent for John and listened to him explain spiritual matters. It is important for us to understand that while we may say things which anger people, their anger must be because of our stand for the truth, not because we are stubborn, rude, unkind, or hypocritical. Would those who dislike you still have to admit you are righteous and holy? Would they value your words even if their initial response was anger? Would they come to you in crisis because they know you love them? They should, if your attitude and actions are like John's. How can you become that kind of a person?

SAY WHAT?
Observation: What do I see?

SO WHAT?
Interpretation: What does it mean?

NOW WHAT?
Application: How does it apply to me?

THEN WHAT?
Implementation: What do I do?

EXTRA READING
MARK 6

ontrack devotions

#ontrackdevos

SAY WHAT?

What reasons do you have for loving God besides what He does for you?

SO WHAT?

In what ways can you show Him how much you love Him today?

NOW WHAT?

How can you avoid having motives similar to the ones we see in this passage?

THEN WHAT?

In light of this passage, what personal commitment can you make?

Do you have friends that seem to only like you because of what you can give them? They like your car, your house, your pool or another possession, and that seems to be their motivation for spending time with you. You know they spend time with you just to get something from you. If you answered yes, then you know exactly how Christ felt in this passage. This chapter ends with a scene that is repeated throughout the Gospels. People flocked to see Jesus because of what He could do for them, not because they loved Him or wanted to spend time with Him. The crowd wanted only what He could give them. Jesus must have longed for those in the crowd to love Him for who He was and not for what He could do. Is your relationship with Christ like the ones in today's reading? Do you only talk to Him in prayer when you need help or want something? Do you ever pray without asking for something? We ought to love Him for who He is, not for what He does for us. Why not spend some time today talking with God about why you love Him? That alone could take hours!

EXTRA READING
MARK 6

The book of Proverbs was designed to help us in "attaining wisdom and discipline; in understanding words of insight; in acquiring a disciplined and prudent life, doing what is right and just and fair; in giving prudence to the simple, knowledge and discretion to the young." As you read through this chapter, write down the verses that are most significant to you in your present circumstances.

VERSE | WHAT TRUTH IT COMMUNICATES | HOW IT IMPACTS MY LIFE

#ontrackdevos

MARK 7:1-13

SAY WHAT?

Observation: What do I see?

SO WHAT?

Interpretation: What does it mean?

NOW WHAT?

Application: How does it apply to me?

THEN WHAT?

Implementation: What do I do?

It is obvious in today's reading that Christ was upset about a specific practice of the Pharisees. What was it exactly, and why was it so terrible? In verse 11, we learn that the Pharisees were compelling people to give an extra amount of money to the temple. This caused hardship on families who needed that extra money to take care of their elderly parents. Any money that they could give to help their parents was given to the Synagogue. Jesus confronted them with setting aside the commands of God in order to observe their own traditions. They deliberately chose to ignore the Word of God and honor the traditions of men instead. God would never ask us to violate one part of Scripture in order to obey another. We must never allow ourselves to justify our sin in this way. We will be held to the standard of God's choosing, not our own. God has clear expectations for our lives and wants us to understand what they are. God provided the Bible for that purpose. Might there be an area of your life in which you have justified your disobedience with an excuse like the one they gave in today's reading? What are you going to do about it?

EXTRA READING

MARK 7

What kind of response does God look for from us? What kind of response was He looking for from people who observed the miracles in today's reading? It was not the one He got. Jesus, in an amazing way, healed the man who was deaf and mute. Think about this miracle. This man had never heard speech before, yet Jesus loosened his tongue so that he could speak. He could suddenly hear and understand and then speak clearly. What a miracle! Jesus asked the man not to tell anyone. However, he did not restrain himself and told his story over and over. Everyone was overwhelmed with amazement. Their response was "He has done everything well", not "He must be God." They saw the miraculous, but it did not compel them to believe that Jesus was the Messiah. Nor did they come to Him to have their sins forgiven. Repentance was not part of their response to His work. Amazement and being overwhelmed is not what God wants. He wants us to respond with repentance and come to Him in humble obedience. Is your response to God the one He wants for your life? Are you amazed but not humbled?

SAY WHAT?
Observation: What do I see?

SO WHAT?
Interpretation: What does it mean?

NOW WHAT?
Application: How does it apply to me?

THEN WHAT?
Implementation: What do I do?

EXTRA READING
MARK 7

 ontrack devotions

 #ontrackdevos

SAY WHAT?
What kind of signs do people look for to determine who God is or what He wants?

SO WHAT?
What signs has God given you to show you His will?

NOW WHAT?
Examine your life. What direction is God moving you in light of what He is currently doing in your life?

THEN WHAT?
In light of this passage, what personal commitment can you make?

What kind of sign do you think the Pharisees had in mind in verse 11? What was it that they wanted Jesus to do that would indicate who He was? Did they want Him to perform a miracle? Did they want Him to do something that no human could possibly do so that they would know for certain that He was God? Would feeding 4,000 people with seven loaves of bread qualify as a sign from heaven? It is unbelievable that they could have seen this amazing sign and yet ask for more. How could they not see that Jesus gave them more than enough evidence to demonstrate who He was. It is obvious that no sign would have convinced them He was the Messiah. How true that is today. People are waiting for God to give them some sign of who He is so they can know whether or not to believe on Him. He gives us signs everywhere and yet they miss them. Some Christians look for signs which tell a direction to go or to give them confidence. God gives clear signs and yet they miss them. Could you be looking for a sign He has already given? What exactly are you waiting for?

EXTRA READING
MARK 8

ontrackdevotions.com

When Peter suggested building three shelters, what was he really asking to do? Think about it for a moment. He saw Jesus transfigured before his eyes, which meant He saw Jesus in His glorified state. Not only that, but he also saw Moses and Elijah who were talking with Jesus. He must have wanted to stay there and find a way to keep it going. That could be why he suggested building the three shelters. He wanted to stay up there and not have to go back to his "mundane" life. He must have wanted the moment to never end. Jesus, however, did not take them up the mountain to stay, but to be affected by the event and then return home to impact their worlds with the message of Christ. We, likewise, will have incredible spiritual moments. We may sense the presence of God at camp or a conference, in church, or during personal devotions in an unusual way. We may even feel like Peter and not want the moment to end, but it must. We must go back to the world God has called us to influence, determined to accomplish the task He has given us. These moments are designed by God to affect us in ways that enable us to better influence our worlds. Have you allowed your moment to do just that?

SAY WHAT?
Observation: What do I see?

SO WHAT?
Interpretation: What does it mean?

NOW WHAT?
Application: How does it apply to me?

THEN WHAT?
Implementation: What do I do?

EXTRA READING
MARK 9

ontrack devotions

#ontrackdevos

SAY WHAT?
Observation: What do I see?

SO WHAT?
Interpretation: What does it mean?

NOW WHAT?
Application: How does it apply to me?

THEN WHAT?
Implementation: What do I do?

What words would you use to describe your prayer life? How similar are your requests to the one made in today's reading by the father of the boy with an evil spirit? He came to Jesus because he hoped He could heal his son. He asked Jesus if He would heal his son, but he added a phrase that Jesus picked up on. You should underline it in your Bible. It is the phrase, "if you can." Jesus responded by repeating this phrase and pointing out to the man that his comment indicated unbelief. The man agreed and pleaded with Jesus to give him faith and help him believe. Jesus did, and the boy was healed. In what ways are you like this father? When you pray, you ask God to move on your behalf but what you really mean is, "if you can." You do not possess the real assurance that God will move but have a "hope-so" kind of attitude. How often could Jesus respond to you by repeating the question, "If you can?" We need to be people who come to the Father with hearts that are filled with confidence and assurance that He can and does accomplish His will. Do you really believe that? If not, why not begin today to ask Jesus to help you overcome your unbelief like this father did?

EXTRA READING
MARK 9

Before leaving this great chapter, let's be reminded of one more important truth. Did you ever notice how God puts what appears to be one simple word in a sentence, and it causes the sentence to take on a whole new meaning? In today's reading, we find one of those words. Jesus was attempting to teach the disciples about being a servant. They had just spent time along the road arguing about who would be the greatest in the kingdom. Each disciple must have tried to present his case as to what made him a likely candidate for greatness. Jesus sat them down and told them that if they wanted to be great, they must be the last. But did you notice the word He used before last in verse 35? He said they must not just be the last, but be the "very" last. They were not to be towards the end or in the middle of the pack, but the "very" last. Is this your attitude? Do you try to always step to the forefront and get all the attention, or do you strive to be the very last? Must you be first in line, or do you let others go before you? As you look at what Jesus said, are you a servant? Use today's questions to help you evaluate how you are doing at being a true servant.

SAY WHAT?
How would someone demonstrate himself to be a servant?

SO WHAT?
How would someone demonstrate that he does not have this attitude?

NOW WHAT?
How can you develop a great desire for a servant's heart?

THEN WHAT?
In light of this passage, what personal commitment can you make?

EXTRA READING
MARK 9

#ontrackdevos

PROVERBS 9

The book of Proverbs was designed to help us in "attaining wisdom and discipline; in understanding words of insight; in acquiring a disciplined and prudent life, doing what is right and just and fair; in giving prudence to the simple, knowledge and discretion to the young." As you read through this chapter, write down the verses that are most significant to you in your present circumstances.

VERSE | WHAT TRUTH IT COMMUNICATES | HOW IT IMPACTS MY LIFE

What does it take to receive eternal life? Can a person earn his way into heaven? In today's reading, we discover the answer to both of these questions. In Jesus' conversation with the rich young man, He reveals an important truth about salvation. If you do not understand it, you can come to some wrong conclusions about what it takes to be saved. The disciples listened to what Jesus said to the rich man and were astonished. If what Jesus said was true, His words would mean that no one could be saved. Jesus answered them by saying that they were right to assume that no one can be saved, if it depends on something we do. We are saved when God moves in our hearts and we respond to it, not by something we do. As believers, we understood our need because God revealed it to us. We chose to accept Christ because God gave us the desire. We realized the need for salvation because God revealed it to us. God must do a work in our hearts for us to be saved. No one can ever earn his way to heaven. It isn't anything we do, but what God does. How humble and thankful we should be for God's gift of salvation. Are you?

SAY WHAT?
Observation: What do I see?

SO WHAT?
Interpretation: What does it mean?

NOW WHAT?
Application: How does it apply to me?

THEN WHAT?
Implementation: What do I do?

EXTRA READING
MARK 10

#ontrackdevos

SAY WHAT?

In what events have you clearly seen the hand of God at work in your life?

SO WHAT?

Looking back at them, what conclusions have you come to about what God was working to accomplish?

NOW WHAT?

How can those experiences help you face current circumstances?

THEN WHAT?

In light of this passage, what personal commitment can you make?

Why did Mark feel that it was important to add the phrase, "which no one has ever ridden" to verse 2? Is that fact significant? This is a remarkable series of events that we can read over and easily miss the significance. Jesus gave instructions to two of His disciples. He told them to go into the village where they would find a colt that had been tied up. Matthew tells us that the mother of the colt was there as well. They were to untie the colt and bring it to Jesus to ride. How did He know it would be there? How did He know that He would have permission to untie and ride the colt? That is a miracle! But, it was not just any colt but one that had never been ridden. It is incredible that Jesus knew that, but even more amazing is that the colt was there just for Him to ride. How did the owner know to keep it from being ridden? God had so clearly worked in the events of people's lives so that this very colt would be there when the disciples came, and it would be kept for Christ. It is inconceivable at times to see how God controls the smallest details of our lives to provide for us and accomplish His will! Use today's questions to help you think through this truth in your own life.

EXTRA READING
MARK 11

What point do you suppose Jesus was trying to make to the Pharisees when He used the parable found in this passage? The point was that the Pharisees responded to God the way the people in the parable responded to the owner of the vineyard. As you read this parable, you can feel the emotion of the events. A land-owner graciously allowed people to farm his land in return for a portion of the crop. He first sent a servant to collect his payment. The people not only refused payment, but beat the servant before sending him back. He continued to send servants to collect payment, and they beat and even killed some of them. The Pharisees and other listeners must have been amazed at the unbelievable cruelty of these people. The land-owner finally sent his son to collect payment. They responded by killing his son with the mistaken idea that they would just take the land. Hearing this parable must have filled the listeners with anger. The Pharisees, however, knew that Jesus was talking about them. But knowing Jesus was speaking to them, they still did not repent. Could you be like the Pharisees? When God speaks to you, do not resist! Are you?

SAY WHAT?
Observation: What do I see?

SO WHAT?
Interpretation: What does it mean?

NOW WHAT?
Application: How does it apply to me?

THEN WHAT?
Implementation: What do I do?

EXTRA READING
MARK 12

ontrack devotions

#ontrackdevos

SAY WHAT?

What words would you use to describe your giving habits?

SO WHAT?

What is the most sacrificial gift you have ever given?

NOW WHAT?

What would need to change to be more like this widow in your giving?

THEN WHAT?

In light of this passage, what personal commitment can you make?

How important is vocabulary? Can one word really make a difference? In today's reading, it makes a powerful illustration even more powerful. Jesus closed this chapter with the illustration of a poor widow who gave money to the treasury. Jesus was so impressed with her giving that He used her as an example to the disciples. His point was that God evaluates your gift by looking at how much you could have given, not by how much you gave. To further illustrate this, Jesus did something fascinating with vocabulary in telling this story. In verse 42, He called her a "poor" widow. The word He used meant that she had something but it was not very much. In verse 43 He again called her a "poor" widow, but He used a different Greek word for poor. This word meant she had nothing. Before she gave, she was poor, but at least had a little. After she gave, she had nothing. How sacrificial are you in your giving? Is the amount you give based on keeping back enough for yourself? How does Jesus respond when He sees what you give, knowing how much you could have given? What needs to change?

EXTRA READING

MARK 12

Think back over your life. What was the worst day you can remember? What is the worst day you have ever heard anyone talk about? Imagine being able to say that the distress you experience in one day was greater than any day that had ever been--not just in your life, but in anyone's life since the beginning of time. That would sure be one terrible day. That is what Mark wants us to understand about the tribulation in this chapter. In today's reading, he gives us details concerning conditions in the tribulation just before Christ returns. He says, in verse 19, that the distress of those days will be "unequaled from the beginning." Think about that for a moment--more distress than was involved in the days of Hitler in Germany. The distress of the tribulation will be greater than the distress of the Great Depression. This distress will be greater than it was in the days when Rome persecuted Christians. This distress will be greater than any time in all of history. How does knowing this is true affect you? Does knowing this truth motivate you to make sure that the people in your world trust Christ and miss those violent days? It should!

SAY WHAT?
Observation: What do I see?

SO WHAT?
Interpretation: What does it mean?

NOW WHAT?
Application: How does it apply to me?

THEN WHAT?
Implementation: What do I do?

EXTRA READING
MARK 13

ontrack devotions

#ontrackdevos

SAY WHAT?
Observation: What do I see?

SO WHAT?
Interpretation: What does it mean?

NOW WHAT?
Application: How does it apply to me?

THEN WHAT?
Implementation: What do I do?

What impact did the events in the beginning of today's reading have on Judas? What impact did they have on the actions he took later that day? Do you think these events put him over the edge? Jesus was sitting at the table and Judas watched as a woman entered the room. She must have appeared very emotional in order for Judas to notice and wonder what she had come to do. To his amazement, she walked over to Jesus, broke the jar of perfume, and poured it on Jesus. The other Gospel accounts record for us that she also wiped the feet of Jesus with her hair. Judas could not begin to understand her actions or Jesus' for allowing it. He did not love Christ the way this woman did. He had not realized how great his need was and how incredible the love of God was for him. He had no feelings of humble gratitude for what Christ had done for him whatsoever. He was following Christ for the money, and what he could get out of the relationship. In his anger, he left and went to the High Priest to offer to betray Jesus. Are you at all like Judas? Is your relationship with Jesus leading you to respond like Judas or like this woman?

EXTRA READING
MARK 14

The book of Proverbs was designed to help us in "attaining wisdom and discipline; in understanding words of insight; in acquiring a disciplined and prudent life, doing what is right and just and fair; in giving prudence to the simple, knowledge and discretion to the young." As you read through this chapter, write down the verses that are most significant to you in your present circumstances.

VERSE | WHAT TRUTH IT COMMUNICATES | HOW IT IMPACTS MY LIFE

ontrack
devotions

#ontrackdevos

SAY WHAT?

What kind of commitments do people make and then neglect to complete?

SO WHAT?

What past commitments has God brought to your mind today that you have not yet honored?

NOW WHAT?

How should you respond today to those commitments?

THEN WHAT?

In light of this passage what personal commitment can you make?

When was the last time someone made a commitment to you and did not follow through on it? How did it make you feel? Imagine how Christ felt as He listened to the disciples make commitments to follow Him to the death, knowing they would all desert Him when the critical moment came to stand with Him. Do you suppose His thoughts went back to the upper room? Do you imagine He thought about how passionately Peter declared that he would die with Him if necessary? Do you think He was reminded of their commitment to stand together as His disciples? It must have hurt to see them choose to save their own skin rather than follow through on their commitments. It must also hurt Him to see us do the exact same thing. We come home from an event excited and committed to have devotions faithfully. We commit to love the unlovely and willingly share the message of salvation to the unsaved. Is it possible you made a commitment this summer that you have already forgot and forsaken? There is still time enough to follow through.

EXTRA READING

MARK 14

ontrackdevotions.com

Of all the events that took place in these verses, which do you think was the hardest for Christ to face? This chapter is filled with incredibly emotional moments. It is amazing to think that Christ went through all that for you and for me. What goes through your mind as you read a chapter like this? Today, why not reflect on what Christ has done for you instead of answering a few questions. Read the chapter again, and use the side of the page to jot down your impressions. Maybe you could write down some feelings you have towards God for what He has done for you. Spend a few moments thanking Him for what He did for you.

EXTRA READING
MARK 15

 ontrack
devotions

 #ontrackdevos

SAY WHAT?
Observation: What do I see?

SO WHAT?
Interpretation: What does it mean?

NOW WHAT?
Application: How does it apply to me?

THEN WHAT?
Implementation: What do I do?

As you read more details about the crucifixion of Christ, what stands out to you? One thing you may have noticed is who was not mentioned. Beginning in verse 40, Mark records who was present during the crucifixion. He tells us that Mary Magdalene and Mary the mother of James were there. He also tells us that these women followed Christ and cared for His needs. But, there is an obvious lack of men on the list. Where were the men? Why would the women be present for and witness His death but not the disciples. It would appear that we have the same problem today. Look around in your church and think about how many men are really taking a stand for Christ and having a significant influence in their world. Look around in the ministries of the church and ask yourself how many men you see actively serving compared to the number of women. We need men to step up and influence people for the cause of Christ. Could you be one of those men who needs to take a stand? What would it take for you to get started? Where would you have been the day that Jesus Christ was crucified? Where you are now? Standing or hiding?

EXTRA READING
MARK 15

ontrackdevotions.com

As you come to the completion of this book, what have you learned? In what ways are you different because you read it? What have you learned about Jesus Christ? How about in this chapter? We have learned that Jesus is concerned when people make mistakes, and He wants them to know He still cares. That's must be why He told Mary to go tell the disciples, "and Peter." This book has been filled with so much. Why not take time to record the impact this book has had in your life. Don't be a hearer of the Word who walks away and forgets what he learned so as to have no impact on his life. Be a doer who can't forget what he learned until it changes him. Use today's questions to help you get started.

SAY WHAT?
Why do you think this book was written?

SO WHAT?
What are key principles you can take with you from this book?

NOW WHAT?
What things about Jesus Christ and His ministry did you learn from reading this book?

THEN WHAT?
What do you need to do so this book changes you?

EXTRA READING
MARK 16

ontrack
devotions

#ontrackdevos

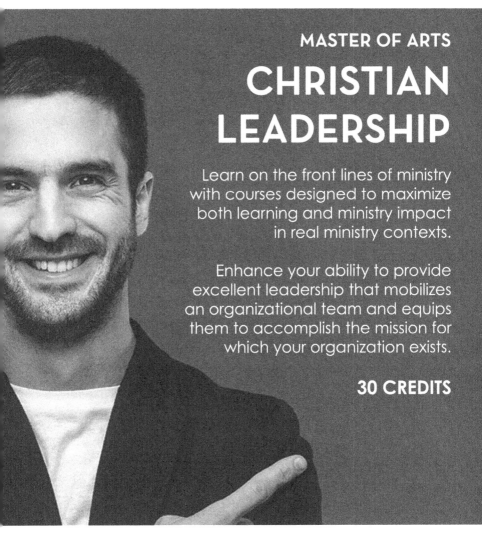

ontrackdevotions.com

(🐦) @ontrackdevos

(f) facebook.com/ontrackdevos

darkness, and the darkness has not overcome it

MONTHLY PRAYER SHEET

"...The prayer of a righteous man is powerful and effective." James 5:16

Reach out...	How I will do it...	How it went...

Other requests...	Answered	How it was answered...

Name: _____

This sheet is designed to help you make personal commitments each month that will help you grow in your walk with God. Fill it out by determining
1. What will push you
2. What you think you can achieve

If you need help filling out your commitments, seek out someone you trust who can help you. Share your commitments with those who will help keep you accountable to your personal commitment.

Personal Devotions:
How did I do with my commitment last month?_____
I will commit to read the OnTrack Bible passage and devotional thought _____ day(s) each week this month.

Church Attendance:
How did I do last month with my attendance? _____
I will attend Youth/Growth Group_____ time(s) this month.
I will attend the Sunday AM service _____ time(s) this month.
I will attend the Sunday PM service _____ time(s) this month.
I will attend_____ time(s) this month.
I will attend_____ time(s) this month.

Scripture Memory:
How did I do with Scripture memory last month? _____
I will memorize _____ key verse(s) from the daily OnTrack Devotions this month.

Outreach:
How did I do last month with sharing Christ? _____
I will share Christ with _____ person/people this month.
I will serve my local church this month by _____
_____

Other Activities:
List any other opportunities such as events, prayer group, etc., that you will participate in this month. _____
_____

ontrack
devotions

#ontrackdevos

Who was the person John referred to as "The Word" in today's reading? It is clear that whoever He was, John believed that He was God. He began by stating that the person he referred to as "The Word", is God. He also stated that John the Baptist would proclaim to all who this man was. John also tells us that although this man was in the world, the world would not recognize Him, but John the Baptist would. His purpose was to prepare the way for Him. The phrase, in verse 15, "He who comes after me has surpassed me because He was before me," provides clear confirmation of who "The Word" is. There was no indication, up through verse 18, of who this man specifically was. But, after reading verse 32, it is made clear. John identified Jesus Christ as the one to whom he referred to as "The Word". We can know that Jesus is God. Therefore, everything John said about "The Word" is true of Jesus. Therefore, if we believe on Him, we can become sons of God. Therefore, Jesus Christ is God. Therefore, we need to respond to Him as God. Have you? Use today's questions to help you evaluate that more closely. Also, have you shared who He is with others?

SAY WHAT?

List the characteristics John gives in this chapter for "The Word," Jesus.

SO WHAT?

How do these descriptions of Jesus affect His ministry in your life?

NOW WHAT?

How can you refer to these attributes when witnessing to unsaved friends?

THEN WHAT?

In light of this passage, what personal commitment should you make?

EXTRA READING
JOHN 1

SAY WHAT?
Observation: What do I see?

SO WHAT?
Interpretation: What does it mean?

NOW WHAT?
Application: How does it apply to me?

THEN WHAT?
Implementation: What do I do?

In this passage, John gives the reader an informative statement about angels. Did you notice it? It is revealed in the conversation that Jesus had with Nathaniel. Jesus touched the life of Philip, and he in turn ran to let his friend Nathaniel know what he had found. At first, Philip was unable to persuade Nathaniel to come to Christ. After some effort, however, he was able to convince Nathaniel to come and investigate Jesus. When Nathaniel arrived, Jesus told him things that no one could have known about him. Nathaniel was amazed. Jesus then told him that he would see even greater evidences of His true nature than what Nathaniel had just seen. Jesus' next statement to Nathaniel revealed information about angels that had not been previously known by anyone. Jesus said that angels are ascending and descending. The obvious implication is that angels are presently on earth, and they go back and forth between heaven and earth. The fact of their constant presence with us on the earth should reassure us. Not only is the Holy Spirit within us and other Christians around us, but there are angels around us as well. What a comfort that should be! We are never alone.

EXTRA READING
JOHN 1

The book of Proverbs was designed to help us in "attaining wisdom and discipline; in understanding words of insight; in acquiring a disciplined and prudent life, doing what is right and just and fair; in giving prudence to the simple, knowledge and discretion to the young." As you read through this chapter, write down the verses that are most significant to you in your present circumstances.

VERSE | WHAT TRUTH IT COMMUNICATES | HOW IT IMPACTS MY LIFE

SAY WHAT?

List some people in your world that you would like to see trust Christ.

SO WHAT?

What are you doing to help them understand their need?

NOW WHAT?

How can today's reading help you in your efforts to influence people for Christ?

THEN WHAT?

In light of this passage, what personal commitment can you make?

What does it require for someone to realize his need for salvation? We often think that it takes the right intellectual comment or illustration. We often believe that if the correct words are spoken in a compelling way, people would trust Christ. In this passage, we are given the explanation of just how one comes to Christ. Jesus performed His first miracle by turning water into wine in this chapter. As John concluded his record of this miracle, he stated that Jesus' disciples put their faith in God "because He revealed His glory." People come to faith in Christ when God reveals to their hearts who Jesus is and what He has done for them. While God often uses our conversations to prompt thoughts, one is saved only through the power of God in his life. It is a work of God that brings people to Christ, not the clever plans of men. We need to be ready to give an answer to anyone at any time as to why we believe in Christ. We also need to have the ability to share the plan of salvation, but we must keep in mind that God is the one who does the work! Have you taken advantage of the opportunities that God has brought to you recently? Are you ready to do so?

EXTRA READING
JOHN 2

ontrackdevotions.com

How do you react when someone receives more attention than you receive? How do you respond when someone gets recognition for what you have done? Hopefully, you are responding as John the Baptist did in the example found in this chapter. John demonstrated incredible humility as he watched his own ministry decrease and Christ's increase. In fact, in today's reading, we see that John's disciples came to him to let him know that Jesus was baptizing people. Their concern was that those whom Jesus baptized were following Him rather than John. People were beginning to overlook John's ministry and follow this new guy, Jesus. Notice John's response in verse 27. John's total confidence was in God. He understood that his calling in life was to prepare the way for Jesus and His ministry. John was content and satisfied to do just that. Would you say your attitude is like John's? Do you trust the Lord and allow Him to use you in any way He wants to, even if it is to make others successful? Or do you always have to be the main guy? What role does God want you to play? Are you willing to play it?

SAY WHAT?
What type of role do you think God wants you to have in your church, workplace, or family?

SO WHAT?
What can you do to begin to fulfill that role more effectively?

NOW WHAT?
How can you avoid being ineffective in that role?

THEN WHAT?
In light of this passage, what personal commitment can you make?

EXTRA READING
JOHN 3

ontrack devotions

#ontrackdevos

SAY WHAT?
Observation: What do I see?

SO WHAT?
Interpretation: What does it mean?

NOW WHAT?
Application: How does it apply to me?

THEN WHAT?
Implementation: What do I do?

Why do people get sick or injured and have bodies that get tired? One answer to that question is found in today's reading. Those things happen so that God can accomplish His purpose in our lives and in the lives of others. Notice the illustration of that in today's reading. Jesus was with His disciples, and they were on their way back to Galilee. They had been ministering in Judea. As they left for home, Jesus made a decision to go through Samaria. As they approached Sychar, Jesus sat down by a well to rest because He was tired from His journey. The disciples went into town but Jesus remained behind. "Just per chance" a woman came to get water from the very well that Jesus was resting by. They began a conversation, and, by the time they were finished, she knew that everyone in town needed to hear more from Christ. Ultimately, many in that town trusted Christ as Savior. If He had not been tired, He would not have stopped, and their conversation would not have taken place. We may never know when our circumstances might be used of God to provide us an opportunity for a conversation like Jesus had with this woman. When it comes, we must be ready to take advantage of it.

EXTRA READING
JOHN 4

ontrackdevotions.com

Why did the townspeople all come out to hear Christ? What did the woman say in order to persuade them to listen? What caused many of them to trust Jesus as Savior? The answer is important for us to keep in mind because it should affect our own methods of outreach. According to verse 39, many of them believed because of the woman's testimony. She went into town and simply told people what she knew, which was what Christ had done for her. She had no training in outreach or evangelism methods. All she knew was that she had met the Lord, and He had changed her life. She wanted them to know what had happened to her so that they could experience the very same thing. We often think we need to have all kinds of training to be able to influence others for Christ. However, if we know Christ as Savior and believe He has changed our lives, then all we ever need to do is simply tell people what God has done in our lives. We just need to share our stories. That is the most powerful tool we have. Use today's questions to help you think through how to share your story with others. Look to share it with someone this week.

SAY WHAT?

In what way is your life different because you know Christ as your Savior?

SO WHAT?

What were the circumstances around your salvation and why did you make that decision?

NOW WHAT?

From your own story, why should someone make the same decision you made?

THEN WHAT?

In light of this passage, what personal commitment can you make?

EXTRA READING
JOHN 4

 ontrack devotions

 #ontrackdevos

SAY WHAT?
Observation: What do I see?

SO WHAT?
Interpretation: What does it mean?

NOW WHAT?
Application: How does it apply to me?

THEN WHAT?
Implementation: What do I do?

One of the purposes of this book is to show people that Jesus Christ is God. Today we see another clear example of the deity of Jesus Christ, and His own claim to be God. It was clear to the Jews, in verse 18 of this chapter, that Jesus' statement to them concerning the healing at the pool was His claim of equality with God. In fact, Jesus knew the crowd understood His statements to be a claim to deity. If Jesus were not God, He would have tried to correct what was an obvious misunderstanding. He did not correct what they heard, but restated it with even more proof. In the remaining verses of this chapter, He gave more evidence to demonstrate that He was in fact, God. He also told them that in order to gain eternal life, they must believe the words He spoke and must believe on Him. How those words must have stung the Jews who refused to accept Christ as the Messiah. How have you responded to Jesus? Do you believe He is God, sent to die for your sins and raised from the dead to give victory over sin? Which friends from school or work need to know who Jesus is and what He has done for them? Are you prepared to share with them? When will you get started?

EXTRA READING
JOHN 5

Why did the people in today's reading want to make Jesus Christ their King? The motivation they demonstrated is one we all need to be careful of having in our relationships with Christ. It seems obvious from the text that the reason they wanted Jesus to be king was because He provided food for them that they did not have to work for. They just watched Him take five loaves and two fish and turn it into enough food to feed over 5,000 people. Imagine what life would be like if this miracle worker were the king! He could meet the material needs of all his people, and they would not have to work for it. Farmers would not have to grow as much food. Providing for one's family would be almost effortless. Life would be great. What they missed was that Jesus Christ wanted them to desire Him as king for different reasons. He wanted to rule their lives, not their land. They wanted material gain, not spiritual power. People often serve Christ and include Him in their lives in order to have their physical needs met. What motivates you? Are you a follower of Christ because you want your spiritual needs met, or simply to have your physical needs taken care of?

SAY WHAT?

What kinds of wrong motivations do people have for following Christ?

SO WHAT?

How can you tell what your motivation is?

NOW WHAT?

What steps can you take to keep your motivation pure?

THEN WHAT?

In light of this passage, what personal commitment can you make?

EXTRA READING
JOHN 6

PROVERBS 12

The book of Proverbs was designed to help us in "attaining wisdom and discipline; in understanding words of insight; in acquiring a disciplined and prudent life, doing what is right and just and fair; in giving prudence to the simple, knowledge and discretion to the young." As you read through this chapter, write down the verses that are most significant to you in your present circumstances.

VERSE | WHAT TRUTH IT COMMUNICATES | HOW IT IMPACTS MY LIFE

What causes someone to recognize who Jesus Christ is and what He has done for him? How does he then trust Christ as his Savior? We realize, after reading these verses, it does not depend on seeing something miraculous. If that was all that were required, everyone fed in today's reading would have trusted Christ. This group of people had just seen Jesus feed 5,000 people with five loaves and two fish. They followed Him across the lake in order to be with Him. They appeared to be ready to accept Christ as the Messiah when they asked in verse 28, "What must we do to do the works God requires?" Jesus told them that all they had to do was believe in the One whom God sent, which He was. Their response was to ask what sign He would give to demonstrate He was the One God sent. He had just fed 5,000 as a sign! What other sign did they need? This illustrates perfectly that salvation is an act of the Holy Spirit on one's heart. An amazing feat is not required for someone to trust Christ. What he really needs is to see the evidence of God's work in our lives and for God to do a work in his heart. As you pray for unsaved people in your world, remember this important truth.

SAY WHAT?
Observation: What do I see?

SO WHAT?
Interpretation: What does it mean?

NOW WHAT?
Application: How does it apply to me?

THEN WHAT?
Implementation: What do I do?

EXTRA READING
JOHN 6

ontrack
devotions

#ontrackdevos

SAY WHAT?

In what ways have you faced opposition from family members?

SO WHAT?

How have you responded to it?

NOW WHAT?

What can you learn from Jesus' response to help you when you face this kind of opposition?

THEN WHAT?

In light of this passage, what personal commitment can you make?

How would it feel to be mocked or ridiculed by the people you love the most? How would it feel to be mocked by not only your brothers and sisters, but also by your parents? How would you feel if you had accomplished something you were proud of, and they laughed at it. How would you feel if, when you made an important decision, they belittled you or doubted your ability to follow through? If any of those situations have happened to you, then you know exactly how Jesus must have felt when those things happened to Him. You should be comforted knowing Jesus understands how you feel. In the beginning of this chapter, we see that Jesus was mocked by His own brothers. Their comment, "You ought to go to Judea so your disciples may see the miracles you do" dripped with sarcasm. That must have hurt the Lord. Unfortunately, sometimes our families are the last ones to believe what God is doing in our lives. Jesus knows how that feels and He wants to encourage and comfort us when we face opposition from those we love. Like Him, do not allow it to deter you from following through. Why not talk to Him about it right now? He understands how you feel.

EXTRA READING
JOHN 7

Why is it important to have correct knowledge of the Scriptures? As today's passage illustrates, it is because incorrect information can cause you to miss God's plan. In these verses, we see the crowd debating whether or not Jesus Christ was the Messiah. They had seen great miracles, and it seemed that there was enough evidence to indicate that He could, in fact, be the Messiah. Their discussion took a negative turn when they came to a conclusion based on inaccurate information. According to verse 27, they decided that Jesus couldn't be the Messiah because they knew that He was from Galilee, and the Messiah could not be from there. The problem with their statement was that it was incorrect. The Old Testament clearly identified where the Messiah would come from so that they would know Him when He came. God did not want the coming of the Messiah to be hard to see. They missed Him because they did not carefully read the Scriptures. They assumed they had the right information, and did not bother to check. Could you be doing the same thing? What truth could you miss either because you do not know the truth or understand it correctly?

SAY WHAT?
Observation: What do I see?

SO WHAT?
Interpretation: What does it mean?

NOW WHAT?
Application: How does it apply to me?

THEN WHAT?
Implementation: What do I do?

EXTRA READING
JOHN 7

ontrack devotions

#ontrackdevos

SAY WHAT?
Observation: What do I see?

SO WHAT?
Interpretation: What does it mean?

NOW WHAT?
Application: How does it apply to me?

THEN WHAT?
Implementation: What do I do?

Have you ever faced something that caused you great fear? Perhaps it was a group of people who wanted to harm you in some way and you worried about what they might say or do. After reading this passage, we see that is the same kind of situation Jesus faced. Jesus was in the temple area, near where the offerings were collected, teaching. He made some very strong statements to the crowd. His statements made the Pharisees very angry, and they wanted to seize Him. But they did not. Why? "Because His time had not yet come." It was not because they did not want to or did not have an opportunity to grab Him, but because the time was not yet right in the plan of God. In other words, the only way that they could carry out their plan was for God to allow it. And, since the time for Jesus' arrest had not arrived, God did not allow the Pharisees to capture Him. People can only do to us what God allows and only when God allows it. Nothing enters our lives without God's permission. We need not fear men, but instead, realize that everything and everyone is under God's control. Remember and take comfort in that today!

EXTRA READING
JOHN 8

ontrackdevotions.com

What does it take to be an effective witness for Christ? What do we need to do in order to be able to lead those in our world to Christ? We have seen it already in this book, and we see it again today. We need to have a story and be able and willing to tell it. In today's reading, Jesus healed a man who was born blind. His blindness was given to him for this very occasion. Through his blindness, God was going to point people to Christ. Jesus healed him which enraged the Pharisees. They sent for his parents who, due to great fear of the religious leaders, were unwilling to say anything. What did the blind man do? He simply told his story. He said, "One thing I do know. I was blind but now I can see!" He didn't give an in-depth Gospel presentation. He also didn't debate them or try to persuade them with clever arguments. He simply explained what God had done for him. God wants Christians today to be willing to simply share what He has done for them. We must let people know that our lives are different because of Christ. Are you ready to tell your story? What's keeping you from sharing it? Pray for opportunities and take the opportunities given.

SAY WHAT?
What has God done in your life since you trusted Christ?

SO WHAT?
What has God done in your life so far this Fall?

NOW WHAT?
How can you tell others what God has done and continues to do in your life?

THEN WHAT?
In light of this passage, what personal commitment can you make?

EXTRA READING
JOHN 9

ontrack
devotions

SAY WHAT?
Observation: What do I see?

SO WHAT?
Interpretation: What does it mean?

NOW WHAT?
Application: How does it apply to me?

THEN WHAT?
Implementation: What do I do?

How secure is our salvation? Is it possible for us to lose our salvation? This chapter gives to us a great illustration of how secure we are in God's mind. It certainly demonstrates that we can never lose our salvation. This entire chapter is devoted to communicating how much Jesus loves us. He knows our names. He never abandons us even during the most difficult times. He always goes before us. All this illustrates His great love. In verses 25-30, He concludes by demonstrating the security He has provided. Jesus tells us that, first of all, we are safe in His hands. They are wrapped around us, and no one can ever take us out of the safety of His hands. But, He does not stop there. He then tells us that the Father has His hands wrapped around Christ's hands to give us even more security. It is like a kid holding a coin with both hands and then having his dad wrap his hands around yours to hold it even tighter. No one can touch us and nothing can ever take us out of those hands. We cannot lose our salvation. It is secure. We are safe within the hands of God the Father and His Son, Jesus. Allow that truth to comfort you today.

EXTRA READING
JOHN 10

The book of Proverbs was designed to help us in "attaining wisdom and discipline; in understanding words of insight; in acquiring a disciplined and prudent life, doing what is right and just and fair; in giving prudence to the simple, knowledge and discretion to the young." As you read through this chapter, write down the verses that are most significant to you in your present circumstances.

VERSE | WHAT TRUTH IT COMMUNICATES | HOW IT IMPACTS MY LIFE

SAY WHAT?

What fears could cause someone to doubt what Christ has said?

SO WHAT?

How might those fears affect someone in the same way that Thomas was affected?

NOW WHAT?

How can Thomas' experience with the Lord help others whose doubt is rooted in fear?

THEN WHAT?

In light of this passage, what personal commitment can you make?

We often hear the disciple Thomas referred to as "Doubting Thomas." Do his comments in today's reading seem to confirm that title? A close look at this dialog would seem to indicate otherwise. Jesus told the disciples that He was going to His friend Lazarus, who had died. The problem with this decision was that Lazarus lived in Bethany and the disciples felt it was too close to Jerusalem to be safe for them. The Jews of Jerusalem were the ones who threatened Jesus and wanted to kill Him. To the disciples, that meant certain death for all of them, and, most importantly, for Christ. In the midst of this discussion, Thomas spoke out in verse 16 and said something remarkable for someone who was supposed to be a doubter. He told the disciples that they should all go together so they could all die with Him. He felt that if Christ were going to die, he would rather die with Him than be left alone. Thomas could not bear the thought of losing Jesus in death. His doubt was not from a lack of faith, but from a fear that Christ would leave him alone. Do you struggle with doubt? Could you, like Thomas, doubt because of fear? Use today's questions to help you determine next steps.

EXTRA READING

JOHN 11

Are there ever negative consequences when God does a miracle in our lives? If we are anything like Lazarus, the answer is yes. Jesus had performed the greatest miracle possible in Lazarus since he had been raised from the dead. As a result, many people believed in Jesus Christ. Word about what had happened to Lazarus spread throughout the country side, and people came from all over to see this man who had been raised from the dead. What an extraordinary opportunity Lazarus had to share his story with others. But in verse 10, we see that not everyone was excited. This miracle put Jesus' critics in a very complicated position because it demonstrated that Jesus was the Messiah. The chief priests hated Lazarus for the problems he caused them and wanted to kill him. Even today, we can face opposition when God does a great work in our hearts. Opposition often comes from those who are in sin and do not want to repent, those who are unsaved, and even those who are jealous of our spiritual journeys. We must tell our story even though not everyone will rejoice with the evidence of God's work. Even the opposition is an opportunity for growth and influence!

SAY WHAT?
Observation: What do I see?

SO WHAT?
Interpretation: What does it mean?

NOW WHAT?
Application: How does it apply to me?

THEN WHAT?
Implementation: What do I do?

EXTRA READING
JOHN 12

SAY WHAT?

List the people in your life you love most.

SO WHAT?

What have you done recently to show them how much you love them?

NOW WHAT?

What can you do this week to demonstrate the "full extent" of your love for them?

THEN WHAT?

In light of this passage, what personal commitment can you make?

If we asked people in your world how much you loved them, what would they say? How have you demonstrated your love to them? In today's reading, there is a phrase that ought to cause everyone of us to examine our love for people. Jesus gathered His disciples together for one final time before His crucifixion. The time had come for God to allow Him to be captured and crucified. Jesus loved these men. In humility, He served them and met their needs. His love for them was so great that He desired to help them any way He could. If that meant washing their dirty feet, then that's what He did. I'm sure they would never forget the events of that evening and how much Jesus loved them. How do you demonstrate your love to those in your world? Do you seek each day to demonstrate in tangible ways the "full extent" of your love for them? Do you serve them so they know you love them? Can you think of a recent "washing of feet" type of demonstration of love on your part? Think of something your can do this week to tangibly show how much you love people.

EXTRA READING
JOHN 13

Have you ever felt totally alone? Have you ever felt as if there isn't anyone who really understands how you feel? That no one can help you? This must be the way the disciples felt at this point in their lives. By this time, they had walked with Jesus for almost three years. One of their great fears had been that He would leave them, and they would have to manage on their own. He sat them down to further explain what would happen, and they realized that He would, in fact, be leaving them. They would be alone just as they feared. They did not understand where He was going or how He would get there. Jesus, sensing their hearts, let them know they would never be alone. He would send the Holy Spirit who would ALWAYS be with them. He would always be there to guide, protect and meet any needs they would have. You see, if we know Christ as our Savior, we are never truly alone. Although people may walk away, He never will. Even if our friends and family are not there to help or understand, He is always there. He is waiting and always available. Take your struggle to Him. Don't allow that to be the last place you go.

SAY WHAT?
Observation: What do I see?

SO WHAT?
Interpretation: What does it mean?

NOW WHAT?
Application: How does it apply to me?

THEN WHAT?
Implementation: What do I do?

EXTRA READING
JOHN 14

ontrack devotions

#ontrackdevos

SAY WHAT?

How can you evaluate how fruitful you are in your walk with God?

SO WHAT?

In what ways has God "picked you up" to make you more fruitful?

NOW WHAT?

In what ways has God "pruned you" to make you more fruitful?

THEN WHAT?

In light of this passage, what personal commitment can you make?

In today's reading, we find a passage that is often used to illustrate that we can lose our salvation. However, if you examine the passage closely, you come to a different conclusion. This passage is about fruitfulness. Christ was explaining what God does to help us become more fruitful. First, someone who bears no fruit God "cuts off." The word "cuts off" here is better translated "picks up." That is also more consistent with the analogy Christ used here. When a vine is not bearing fruit, the first thing a gardener does is pick it up off the ground so it can bear fruit more easily. Second, when we bear some fruit, God prunes us so we can bear more fruit. Finally, if we want to bear much fruit, then we must remain in Christ, to stay consistent in our walk with Him. Verse 6 tells us that if, after all God has done, we still remain unfruitful, then we may be picked up, thrown out, and burned. According to 1 Corinthians 3:15, it is our "works" that will be burned up, but we will be saved. The point of this passage? God does everything needed for us to bear fruit, so there is no reason why we shouldn't. Are you? Use today's questions to help you examine yourself.

EXTRA READING
JOHN 15

Have you ever had an experience that was difficult and very painful? You hated the situation at first and may have even tried to change it. Then you began to see the good it was accomplishing, and your whole attitude about it changed? Today we find a similar example in the lives of the disciples. They were in the upper room with Jesus, and He was spending His final moments with them. As we mentioned earlier, He was preparing them for the events that were about to unfold. They were discouraged and filled with grief. He told them, though, that these events were really for their good. The events of His future must take place so that something better would happen. They had Jesus with them, which was the best possible scenario. They did not realize that His death would result in the arrival of the Holy Spirit. The events about to unfold would be very painful, but the disciples would be stronger because of them. Likewise, we must keep that in mind in our daily living. God brings events in our lives to strengthen us and make us better able to serve Him. Are you facing a painful situation right now? Let Jesus' words today encourage you. There is a plan!

SAY WHAT?
Observation: What do I see?

SO WHAT?
Interpretation: What does it mean?

NOW WHAT?
Application: How does it apply to me?

THEN WHAT?
Implementation: What do I do?

EXTRA READING
JOHN 16

ontrack devotions

PROVERBS 14

The book of Proverbs was designed to help us in "attaining wisdom and discipline; in understanding words of insight; in acquiring a disciplined and prudent life, doing what is right and just and fair; in giving prudence to the simple, knowledge and discretion to the young." As you read through this chapter, write down the verses that are most significant to you in your present circumstances.

VERSE | WHAT TRUTH IT COMMUNICATES | HOW IT IMPACTS MY LIFE

As you read the prayer of Jesus in today's passage, what phrases caught your attention? Did you notice what He said in verse 6? He made an amazing statement that very few of us could make at the end of our lives. Jesus spent His final hours in prayer with His heavenly Father. It was an emotional time for Him. He knew the guards were coming soon to lead Him away to be crucified. He began His prayer by telling the Father, "I have revealed you to those whom you gave me out of the world." There were some whom God had placed into the world, and Jesus had revealed the Father to them. What a statement! Could you make a statement like that? God has given to you a group of people on your athletic team. Have you revealed the Father to them? God has placed you in your work place with individuals who need Him. Have you revealed the Father to them? You attend school with kids who sit by you in math or history or keyboarding. Have you revealed the Father to them? Your home is surrounded by a neighborhood of people. Have you revealed the Father to them? Use today's questions to help you get started.

SAY WHAT?

Write down the names of people in your world who need for you to reveal the Father to them.

SO WHAT?

What have you done to reveal the Father to them?

NOW WHAT?

How can you do a better job of revealing the Father to them?

THEN WHAT?

In light of this passage, what personal commitment can you make?

EXTRA READING
JOHN 17

#ontrackdevos

SAY WHAT?
How can you tell what someone's motivation is?

SO WHAT?
What motivations do you see in your own life?

NOW WHAT?
What can you do to keep your motives pure?

THEN WHAT?
In light of this passage, what personal commitment can you make?

What is your motivation for living the lifestyle that you do? Why do you have your devotions? Why do you go to church? Hopefully, as you examine your life closely, you find that your motivation is not like that of the Pharisees in today's reading. In the midst of the crucifixion story, we find an unbelievable comment that demonstrates just how wicked these people were. They were trying to have Jesus crucified, and they were in a big hurry. Why? According to verse 28, it was so they could get home quickly to eat the Passover meal. It was not because they strongly believed in seeing justice served. It wasn't because they, out of pure devotion, were seeking to follow the laws of God. It was not out of love for those who may follow Him. They didn't want it to interfere with their plans. Too often, we are just like these people in our service to God. We make decisions based on our own selfish desires, not on what we really believe God wants. We say we are committed, but in reality, we just want something for ourselves, like comfort or a good reputation. Could that be your motivation? Examine yourself to see!

EXTRA READING
JOHN 18

ontrackdevotions.com

This book was written to illustrate to its readers that Jesus Christ is, in fact, God. We have seen throughout this book many examples to prove the deity of Christ. What is written in today's reading that would convince you that Jesus is God? What about His love for people in the midst of His own pain. He was on the cross with nails in His hands and feet. He had already been beaten, tortured and denied. Yet, in spite of His own pain, He looked down at His mother and passed the responsibility of her care to John. He was thinking of others while He Himself was in pain. Then He died. His death was not according to the Pharisees schedule or as a result of their torture. He died by surrendering His spirit up to the Father. He died according to God's plan. Every detail of this chapter reveals that Jesus Christ was no ordinary man. He was God, and He illustrated who He was even in the midst of His greatest pain and suffering. He did all this for us--that we might have forgiveness of sins. Who in your world needs to know who Jesus Christ is and what He has done for them? Create a plan for sharing Christ with him. Pray for the opportunity and then take it!

SAY WHAT?
Observation: What do I see?

SO WHAT?
Interpretation: What does it mean?

NOW WHAT?
Application: How does it apply to me?

THEN WHAT?
Implementation: What do I do?

EXTRA READING
JOHN 19

ontrack devotions

#ontrackdevos

As you looked at today's Bible reading passage you no doubt thought there was a typo since this is the same passage we read yesterday. It is not, however, a mistake. This chapter is the account of what Jesus went through for you. What amazing love Jesus Christ demonstrated to us! It is too important of a passage to just read quickly and move on. We want to emphasize again the price He paid, so we are reading this chapter again today. Instead of taking time to read a devotional thought, or write out answers to questions on the side of this page, go back to the passage and at the end of every verse think to yourself, "for me." Example: Then Pilate took Jesus and had him flogged, (for me). Also, ask yourself, "How should I respond to such love?" In what way can you show Him today how thankful you are for what He has done for you?

EXTRA READING
JOHN 19

Who are the people that Jesus was referring to when He spoke to Thomas in verse 29? It might encourage you to know that it is those of us living now who have trusted Christ as Savior. Thomas was not present when Jesus had appeared earlier to the disciples. As a result, he allowed the pain of losing Jesus in death to prevent him from believing that He might really be alive. Jesus came to Thomas and clearly showed him that He had, in fact, risen from the dead. Jesus also told him to touch His side and hands to prove that He was really Jesus. Only when Thomas saw Christ personally did he believe. Jesus told Thomas that because he saw Him he believed, but it is even more blessed to believe even though we have not seen Him with our own eyes. You and I, who have trusted Christ, have done so in faith. We have not physically seen the Lord or have been able to do what Thomas did. We have never touched His hands or side, yet we still believe. Christ commends us for our faith and lets us know that He is pleased with us. Faith is being sure of what we cannot see physically. How great it will be when we finally can see Christ, when we can touch Him and worship. Will you be ready?

SAY WHAT?
Observation: What do I see?

SO WHAT?
Interpretation: What does it mean?

NOW WHAT?
Application: How does it apply to me?

THEN WHAT?
Implementation: What do I do?

EXTRA READING
JOHN 20

ontrack devotions

#ontrackdevos

SAY WHAT?
Observation: What do I see?

SO WHAT?
Interpretation: What does it mean?

NOW WHAT?
Application: How does it apply to me?

THEN WHAT?
Implementation: What do I do?

Why does John tell us exactly how many fish they caught in today's reading? Does it really make any difference? It does if the author wants to again remind us that the purpose of the book is that we might know that Jesus is the Son of God. John emphasized that what happened was not due to good fortune that morning. It was not because of Peter's expertise in fishing. It was a miracle. It could not be explained in any other way except as a great work of God. Jesus told them to put down their nets. They did and caught 153 fish. Also interesting, is what John said as he closed this book. Jesus, in the presence of the disciples, had done many other miraculous signs not recorded in John's account. In fact, if John would have tried to record everything that had taken place with Christ, there would not be enough space in all the world to store the books. It is so incredible to read this book and realize we do not even scratch the surface of all Christ did. After concluding this book, who do you believe Jesus Christ is? How have you responded to that knowledge? Ask God to reveal to your heart who He is and the depth of His love. Who else needs to know Who He is?

EXTRA READING
JOHN 21

WILDERNESS OUTFITTING

The longest-standing tool in our toolbox, the **Wilderness Outfitting** program presents an opportunity for the intentional leader to gain abnormal access to **real connection** with those they lead.

The wilderness can be leveraged into significant access to **real relationships** and **real conversations** that defy other environments... and it transfers back home beautifully.

LEARN MORE AT
SIMPLYAPILGRIM.COM/TRIPS

Photos by **Katie Hall** from a 2016 Pilgrimage trip with Ogletown Baptist Church (DE).

katiehallcreative.com

BUT YOU WILL RECEIVE POWER
WHEN THE HOLY SPIRIT COMES
ON YOU, AND YOU WILL BE MY
WITNESSES IN JERUSALEM, AND
IN ALL JUDEA AND SAMARIA,
AND TO THE ENDS OF THE
EARTH. ACTS 1:8 (NIV)

DECEMBER
2019
ACTS

MONTHLY PRAYER SHEET

"...The prayer of a righteous man is powerful and effective." James 5:16

Reach out...	How I will do it...	How it went...

Other requests...	Answered	How it was answered...

Name: _____

This sheet is designed to help you make personal commitments each month that will help you grow in your walk with God. Fill it out by determining
      1. What will push you
      2. What you think you can achieve
If you need help filling out your commitments, seek out someone you trust who can help you. Share your commitments with those who will help keep you accountable to your personal commitment.

Personal Devotions:
How did I do with my commitment last month?_____
I will commit to read the OnTrack Bible passage and devotional thought _____ day(s) each week this month.

Church Attendance:
How did I do last month with my attendance? _____
I will attend Youth/Growth Group_____ time(s) this month.
I will attend the Sunday AM service _____ time(s) this month.
I will attend the Sunday PM service _____ time(s) this month.
I will attend_____ time(s) this month.
I will attend_____ time(s) this month.

Scripture Memory:
How did I do with Scripture memory last month? _____
I will memorize_____ key verse(s) from the daily OnTrack Devotions this month.

Outreach:
How did I do last month with sharing Christ?_____
I will share Christ with _____ person/people this month.
I will serve my local church this month by _____
_____

Other Activities:
List any other opportunities such as events, prayer group, etc., that you will participate in this month._____
_____

ontrack
devotions

#ontrackdevos

How can you tell if you are growing spiritually? As you look back over this past year, how can you determine if this year has been a year of growth? You could use the examples of growth in the lives of the apostles found in this passage as a guide. They were once fearful, but conquered fear and replaced it with boldness. They were impatient and moved ahead of God. However, with growth, they waited for God to give direction. In fact, the text says that they prayed constantly. These were the same guys who had asked Jesus to teach them to pray. Obviously, they had learned well. These were the guys who had fallen asleep in the garden when they were there with Christ. They weren't sleeping in this chapter. When they had to decide who to replace Judas with, they asked God to guide them. They had changed so much since the days when they fought over who would be the greatest. What evidence do you see of your spiritual growth? Can you make similar observations to the ones we have seen in the lives of the disciples? Why not take the time to go through today's questions to see just how far you have grown.

SAY WHAT?

In what areas of your life have you seen spiritual growth this past year?

SO WHAT?

What were some of the spiritual highlights from this past year?

NOW WHAT?

What will you need to do to see continued growth in those areas?

THEN WHAT?

In light of this passage, what personal commitment can you make?

EXTRA READING
ACTS 1

#ontrackdevos

SAY WHAT?

Observation: What do I see?

SO WHAT?

Interpretation: What does it mean?

NOW WHAT?

Application: How does it apply to me?

THEN WHAT?

Implementation: What do I do?

How do you think the people in your church would respond if God began to move in a miraculous way as He did in the life of the early church? Would everyone be excited or would there be opposition? That is the one response we often forget to consider, as we see in verse 13. God was obviously moving in this church. In fact, as you continue to read this chapter, you will see that ultimately 3,000 people trusted Christ as a result of what God was doing. One could assume that everyone would be enthusiastic and excited. You would think unity would abound among the believers, and everyone would want to be part of what God was doing. However, some made fun of what was happening and even accused the apostles of being drunk. Even in the early church there were people who opposed what God was doing. You also should expect opposition when God begins to work. As God works in your life to use you to influence others towards greater Christ-likeness, understand that not everyone will be happy. Some will make fun of you and oppose you. Be ready for it and determine to respond in a way that honors and pleases God.

EXTRA READING
ACTS 2

ontrackdevotions.com

What can we learn from the example of Peter and John in today's reading? Is it something you can apply to your life today? What was intended to be a simple trip to the temple to pray, turned into a major opportunity to share Christ with a large group of people. The chapter began with a beggar being healed and ended with Peter preaching to the masses. Why? First, Peter and John used what God had given them to impact this man. They told him they had no silver or gold, but, what they did have, they would give to him. Likewise, we need to influence people by using whatever God has given to us. Second, they seized the opportunity to share Christ. They did not seek it or create it, but when it came, they took full advantage of the moment. Likewise, we need to make sure to seize the opportunities that God gives to us to share Christ each and every day. Third, they were prepared to share their faith. Are you? If someone came up to you this afternoon and asked how to be saved, could you tell them? Make sure to use what God has given you, take advantage of opportunities, and be ready to share when opportunities come.

SAY WHAT?
Observation: What do I see?

SO WHAT?
Interpretation: What does it mean?

NOW WHAT?
Application: How does it apply to me?

THEN WHAT?
Implementation: What do I do?

EXTRA READING
ACTS 3

 ontrack devotions

 #ontrackdevos

SAY WHAT?

What words would people use to describe you?

SO WHAT?

What about your life demonstrates you have been with Jesus?

NOW WHAT?

How can you do a better job of demonstrating you have been with Jesus?

THEN WHAT?

In light of this passage, what personal commitment can you make?

What do people observe about you when they spend time with you? If we talked to the people you spent time with over the past week, what would they tell us about you? Hopefully, they would say what was said about the apostles in today's reading. Peter and John were called before the religious rulers. They were asked questions about what they were saying to the people and by whose authority they said it. Peter saw this as an opportunity to share Christ. It seems the lessons Peter learned from his experience with the servant girl in the courtyard had made a great difference in his life. Unlike then, Peter was controlled by the Holy Spirit, and with great courage he took a stand and shared Christ with these men. These men were so impressed by his words that they said, "these men had been with Jesus." It was obvious from Peter's behavior that he knew Christ and had spent time with Him. Is it obvious that you know the Lord? Do people who spend time with you walk away saying that you must spend time with Christ? If not, what would need to change for them to say those things? Remember, even if you have denied Christ in the past, you could change, and people can notice!

EXTRA READING

ACTS 4

What reaction does your community have to what is taking place in your church? Do the events of this past week cause them to laugh or be amazed? Have the events that have taken place in your youth group caused others to want to be a part of your group or want to avoid it? Does the description of the early church in verse 11 ever describe your church? This was a church that those in the community noticed. Not because of the wrong things that went on, but because of the right things. As a result, verse 11 tells us that great fear gripped the church and everyone who heard about what was taking place. In this case, they heard that people in that church took sin seriously. What is your church known for in the community? When people hear the name of your church, what thoughts do you think come to their minds? When your friends find out what church you attend, what response do they have? Do they want to attend? What would need to change in order for your church to be known for what this church was known for? What can you do to help your church have a positive reputation in the community? How can you begin to change!

SAY WHAT?
Observation: What do I see?

SO WHAT?
Interpretation: What does it mean?

NOW WHAT?
Application: How does it apply to me?

THEN WHAT?
Implementation: What do I do?

EXTRA READING
ACTS 5

ontrack devotions

SAY WHAT?
Observation: What do I see?

SO WHAT?
Interpretation: What does it mean?

NOW WHAT?
Application: How does it apply to me?

THEN WHAT?
Implementation: What do I do?

Today, we are introduced to a great man of God who influenced the early church. In fact, he is the main character of the next three chapters in the book of Acts. His name is Stephen. Stephen was a man who had an unbelievable impact on the lives of people. He was known to be full of wisdom and the Spirit by the people in his world. As a result of his life and death, the message of the gospel was scattered all over the world and the Apostle Paul was saved. What is amazing about his story is his ministry in the early church. You might think he had a significant leadership kind of ministry. But in reality, he did not. According to verses 1-6, a group of Jewish widows in the church were overlooked in the distribution of the food. Stephen was one of the men chosen to deliver food to the widows. Doesn't sound like an important job. What it reveals to us is that we do not have to have the so-called "leadership positions" to be able to influence people for Christ. We all can influence individuals by being the kind of person Stephen was no matter what "position" we might hold. Being a leader is not about a position. It is about having an influence. How can you begin influencing people today?

EXTRA READING
ACTS 6

As you read today's passage and reflect on yesterday's reading, what qualities do you see in Stephen that enabled him to have such a great influence on his world? First, you notice that he knew the Word of God. To be able to recount Biblical history as he did in chapter 7, he must have been a man who spent a lot of time in the Scriptures. Second, we see him as a man who used good judgment. People viewed him as being wise and probably went to him when they needed to talk to someone. Third, he was godly. People knew he was a man who was filled with the Holy Spirit. His love for God and commitment to Him must have been obvious. Fourth, he showed great courage. He was not afraid to tell people the truth, even if it made them angry at him. Fifth, he had great compassion. How else could a man, while being stoned, ask God to forgive the very people who where throwing the rocks. With these qualities, he could influence people even though he didn't have a "leadership position." How do you compare to Stephen? What can you do to become more like him? Use today's questions to help you get started influencing people no matter what your position is.

SAY WHAT?
Which of the five characteristics mentioned of Stephen do you see in yourself?

SO WHAT?
Which of the five do you need to develop more fully?

NOW WHAT?
How can you begin to do so?

THEN WHAT?
In light of this passage, what personal commitment should you make?

EXTRA READING
ACTS 7

ontrack devotions

#ontrackdevos

PROVERBS 15

The book of Proverbs was designed to help us in "attaining wisdom and discipline; in understanding words of insight; in acquiring a disciplined and prudent life, doing what is right and just and fair; in giving prudence to the simple, knowledge and discretion to the young." As you read through this chapter, write down the verses that are most significant to you in your present circumstances.

VERSE | WHAT TRUTH IT COMMUNICATES | HOW IT IMPACTS MY LIFE

Why, when the church was scattered, did the apostles stay behind in Jerusalem? Is there a lesson we can learn from these circumstances? Could it be that God is trying to show us again what we have seen with Stephen's life? Could it have been God's design to show us He does not always use the "big guys" to influence people? Notice, not only did the early church members scatter after Stephen's death, but they left Jerusalem with great boldness in their witness. In verse 4, we are told that these people preached the Word wherever they went. God even gives us an example of how they specifically influenced their worlds. Philip, not the disciple but one of the men chosen to distribute food in chapter 6, went to Samaria and began to proclaim Christ. As a result, many trusted Him as Savior. He was also led by God to speak to an Ethiopian man who received Christ. These were ordinary people who just used what they had to let others know the message of Christ. Could God be trying to send you the same message? What is keeping you from having an influence in your world? God has always delighted in using ordinary people just like you.

SAY WHAT?
Observation: What do I see?

SO WHAT?
Interpretation: What does it mean?

NOW WHAT?
Application: How does it apply to me?

THEN WHAT?
Implementation: What do I do?

EXTRA READING
ACTS 8

SAY WHAT?
Who has God been prompting you to reach out to?

SO WHAT?
What has your response been? Why?

NOW WHAT?
How can you submit to God's leading in this area?

THEN WHAT?
In light of this passage, what personal commitment can you make?

When was the last time God prompted your heart to reach out to someone? How did you respond? What were the results? Today, we are again reminded of the need to respond immediately to the prompting of God as we never know the plan He has in mind. First, Ananias was asked by God to reach out to Paul. He was afraid and hesitated at first. But because Ananias obeyed God's prompting, Paul received Christ as his Savior. Later, we see that Barnabas responded to the prompting of God also. Paul left for Jerusalem to join the disciples there, but they were afraid of him and would have nothing to do with him. God prompted Barnabas' heart, and he brought Paul to them and spoke to the disciples on his behalf. The results? Paul was encouraged, taught, and ultimately was used by God to take the gospel to the world. Would the results have been the same if any of these men had not responded to the prompting of God? Who has God been prompting you to reach out to? What is keeping you from acting upon God's leading? We must never allow our fears to prevent us from reaching out to the people God is prompting us about. Are you?

EXTRA READING
ACTS 9

ontrackdevotions.com

How does God communicate to us that He wants us to reach out to someone? The example of Peter helps us understand how God might communicate to us that we ought to reach out to someone. Peter was waiting for his meal to be prepared as an invited guest in someone's home. While he waited, God communicated something to his heart which Peter didn't understand at first. As he thought about it, the Spirit of God told him that he needed to go with the men who were coming to find him. When Peter felt prompted, he communicated with God to gain clarification. Today, we communicate with God through prayer. When we sense God would have us reach out to someone, like Peter, we should go to God in prayer. It might be when we hear a message or read a passage and wonder if God is prompting our hearts. When that happens, we must spend time in prayer and allow the Spirit to reveal or confirm His plan to our hearts. Too often, we are not spending time with God in the Word or in prayer so we are not even prepared to be prompted. We must be people who are able to be prompted and respond correctly when we are. Are you?

SAY WHAT?
Observation: What do I see?

SO WHAT?
Interpretation: What does it mean?

NOW WHAT?
Application: How does it apply to me?

THEN WHAT?
Implementation: What do I do?

EXTRA READING
ACTS 10

SAY WHAT?
Observation: What do I see?

SO WHAT?
Interpretation: What does it mean?

NOW WHAT?
Application: How does it apply to me?

THEN WHAT?
Implementation: What do I do?

Have you ever been in a situation in which you attempted to clearly share the gospel with someone but he just was not interested? If so, then you will find today's reading helpful. We see that as the church was being scattered throughout the world, Christians were sharing the gospel only with Jews, even though God had told them to take it to the entire world. However, some of the men began to share the gospel with Greeks also. According to verse 21, a great number of Greeks responded to the message of Christ. The Christians had spent a great deal of time and energy trying to share the gospel with people who were not interested when a group of people who were anxious to know about Christ were close by. We too, can spend significant amounts of time trying to reach people who are not responding and miss those who are waiting to hear. Could there be people in your world who would listen, if you took time to talk to them? Look around, maybe they are on your team or in one of your classes. Ask God to lead you to people around you who are ready to hear God's message. You might be surprised who they are.

EXTRA READING
ACTS 11

When was the last time your church spent time in prayer about a great concern? What would happen if your youth group began to pray for something like the early church did in this chapter? We would see God move in miraculous ways just like He did for them. Peter was in jail, and the entire church began to pray about it. It wasn't just put on a prayer list and mentioned at services. It was not given to the members of a prayer chain. These people spent a lot of time together asking God to move on Peter's behalf. Today's reading tells us they earnestly prayed for him. As a result, God heard and answered. They devoted their time to come together and go before the throne of God on Peter's behalf. How about your own personal prayer life? Are you praying about anything earnestly? Maybe the reason God is not at work in your heart or in your church is because you and others are not praying "earnestly." What would it take for your church to become like the one recorded here? What can you do to see that it takes place? Use today's questions to get started.

SAY WHAT?
What words would you use to describe your prayer life? Your church's prayer life?

SO WHAT?
What would it take to change it into one more like this church's?

NOW WHAT?
What can you do to see those things begin to happen?

THEN WHAT?
In light of this passage, what personal commitment can you make?

EXTRA READING
ACTS 12

ontrack devotions

SAY WHAT?
Observation: What do I see?

SO WHAT?
Interpretation: What does it mean?

NOW WHAT?
Application: How does it apply to me?

THEN WHAT?
Implementation: What do I do?

There is a phrase in today's reading that gives an indication to us of how far the gospel had penetrated the world in the early church days. Did you notice it? It is found in verse 1. There is a list of prophets and teachers of the early church in the beginning of this chapter. One of the names comes with additional information. In verse 1, a man by the name of Manaen is identified. This man had been brought up with Herod, the tetrarch. Manaen was Herod's foster brother. This is the Herod who ruled during the earthly ministry of Christ. It makes you wonder how Manaen heard the gospel and how his decision impacted his brother, Herod. One can only imagine the circumstances involved in this fascinating fact. Here again is evidence of the grace of God working in someone's life, regardless of where he is or who he is related to. When we get to heaven, it will be exciting to talk to him and hear about the circumstances surrounding his conversion. It should also motivate us to take advantage of every opportunity we have to share Christ. We never know what God will do with our efforts. Look for an opportunity to share your faith today.

EXTRA READING
ACTS 13

ontrackdevotions.com

The book of Proverbs was designed to help us in "attaining wisdom and discipline; in understanding words of insight; in acquiring a disciplined and prudent life, doing what is right and just and fair; in giving prudence to the simple, knowledge and discretion to the young." As you read through this chapter, write down the verses that are most significant to you in your present circumstances.

VERSE | WHAT TRUTH IT COMMUNICATES | HOW IT IMPACTS MY LIFE

ACTS 14:8-20

SAY WHAT?
Observation: What do I see?

SO WHAT?
Interpretation: What does it mean?

NOW WHAT?
Application: How does it apply to me?

THEN WHAT?
Implementation: What do I do?

Have you ever experienced a situation in which someone's feelings towards you seemed to change overnight? One minute he loves you, and the next, he can't stand you? If so, you can identify with Paul and Barnabas in today's reading. Paul did some incredible miracles in Lystra. The crowd was convinced Paul and Barnabas were gods. In fact, they were so sure Paul and Barnabas were gods, that they began their preparations to offer sacrifices to them in the temple. Moments later however, some stoned Paul and left him for dead. This passage reminds us of how fickle people can be. If Paul's main concern was pleasing people and he always worried about what they were thinking, he would never have impacted people the way he did. Could the same thing be said of you? The only thing in this world we can count on is the love of God. We need to be committed to what's right even if it means people change how they feel about us. Although it is disappointing and painful, we must never let how others feel about us keep us from doing God's will. Could you be allowing the feelings of others to keep you from doing what is right?

EXTRA READING
ACTS 14

ontrackdevotions.com

What is the difference between a disagreement and division? Can you have one without the other? In today's reading, we learn about a major disagreement between two very godly people, Paul and Barnabas. While their positions were strong and caused them to each go a different way, it did not cause division among the body of Christ. Both where commended by the church and sent out. Disagreement occurs when two people feel differently about an issue. It can be over something very small or something very large. A disagreement can involve only a little emotion or a great deal of emotion. However, we must never allow a disagreement to lead to division. Division occurs when people become angry, refuse to talk to someone, leave to go to another church, etc. All too often we disagree with someone about an issue and find ourselves drawing lines of division which is never right. We need to realize that disagreements occur all the time, but we need to see them for what they are, two different views. Has a disagreement caused division in your family or with your friends? What can you do to change it?

SAY WHAT?
What disagreements have you had recently?

SO WHAT?
How did you respond to the disagreement?

NOW WHAT?
How can you prevent it from leading to a division?

THEN WHAT?
In light of this passage, what personal commitment can you make?

EXTRA READING
ACTS 15

ontrack devotions

#ontrackdevos

SAY WHAT?
Observation: What do I see?

SO WHAT?
Interpretation: What does it mean?

NOW WHAT?
Application: How does it apply to me?

THEN WHAT?
Implementation: What do I do?

How much of an impact does your background have on your destiny? There are some who believe that their backgrounds "determine" their destinies. If that were true, today's passage would be very different. This chapter shows us that our background does not determine our destiny. For example, Timothy came from a mixed race family. His father was Greek and his mother a Jew. In the culture of the day, he would have found life more difficult than mixed race children might today. Also, he had a saved mother and an unsaved father. In fact, some believe that Timothy's father died while he was still young. In spite of all those negative factors, he still became a man greatly used by God. God brought Paul into his life to disciple and train him for ministry. Timothy did great things to further the cause of Christ. His background was used by God to make him a man God could use. Do you wonder if your background could prohibit you from future ministry? Never allow Satan to use your background to cause you to think God would never use you! It has been given to you and will be used by God! He designed it so embrace it.

EXTRA READING
ACTS 16

In what way is your church like the Berean church seen in this chapter? It is a great compliment for a church to be compared to and found to have the same qualities as the church in Berea. Berea was no ordinary church. It was a church that received Paul's message with great eagerness. The people in this church did not come because it was required of them. They didn't complain that church was boring. These were people who sat with eager hearts, ready to be taught God's Word. They were also known as a church who examined God's Word themselves to see if what they were being taught was true. They didn't just depend on Paul to tell them the truth, but searched the Word themselves to discover the truth. It really would be exciting to be part of a church like this. Sadly, it seems few churches can really say this about themselves. Do people in your church come eager to hear a message from the Word of God? Do they spend time individually in the Word studying it for themselves? Do you? Can the qualities of the Berean church be seen in your life? What would need to change for you and your church to be like Berea?

SAY WHAT?
Observation: What do I see?

SO WHAT?
Interpretation: What does it mean?

NOW WHAT?
Application: How does it apply to me?

THEN WHAT?
Implementation: What do I do?

EXTRA READING
ACTS 17

 ontrack devotions

 #ontrackdevos

SAY WHAT?
Observation: What do I see?

SO WHAT?
Interpretation: What does it mean?

NOW WHAT?
Application: How does it apply to me?

THEN WHAT?
Implementation: What do I do?

As you read through this chapter, who do you notice as having the most significant influence? Was it Paul, the preacher and church planter? After all, if he hadn't gone to Corinth, the church would not even have existed there. He had spent countless hours preaching and teaching there. What about Apollos? He was gifted as a communicator and was greatly used by God to impact the lives of many. How can we measure his impact on the church of Ephesus? There are however, two people who could easily go unnoticed, but whose impact may have been even more significant than the two we have already mentioned. Who are they? Priscilla and Aquila. These were two people with whom Paul spent considerable time. They made tents together and no doubt had encouraged him and gave him strength to press on. Apollos was a great preacher, but it was Priscilla and Aquila who took him in and helped him better understand what Christ had done. Often, the most important people are the ones you might not notice. What "unimportant" job has God called you to do? Are you doing it in a way to touch the lives of others?

EXTRA READING
ACTS 18

ontrackdevotions.com

What percentage of people in your town have heard the gospel? How many people, would you guess, know that Jesus Christ died and rose again to save them from their sin? What percentage of kids in your school would know how to receive eternal life and what it really means? How many kids at work know what Christ has done for them and how to receive His gift? Paul answers that question for the province of Asia in verse 10. Did you notice it? Paul's travels spreading the news of Jesus Christ are recorded in the beginning of this chapter. He entered synagogues and boldly proclaimed the news of Christ. He led discussions daily in the lecture hall of Tyrannus. How successful were these efforts? According to verse 10, these efforts resulted in "ALL" the Jews and Greeks, who lived in the province of Asia, hearing the Word of the Lord. That is incredible! One hundred per cent of the Asian Jews and Greeks had been impacted by his efforts. What are you doing to make sure everyone in your world hears the gospel? Are you letting the kids at your school know what Jesus Christ has done for them? Are you sharing Christ at work? When are you going to begin?

SAY WHAT?

How would you describe your efforts to communicate the message of Christ in your world?

SO WHAT?

List ways that you can effectively share what Christ has done.

NOW WHAT?

What action can you take right now to let more people from your world know the message of Christ?

THEN WHAT?

In light of this passage, what personal commitment can you make?

EXTRA READING
ACTS 19

ontrack devotions

#ontrackdevos

PROVERBS 17

The book of Proverbs was designed to help us in "attaining wisdom and discipline; in understanding words of insight; in acquiring a disciplined and prudent life, doing what is right and just and fair; in giving prudence to the simple, knowledge and discretion to the young." As you read through this chapter, write down the verses that are most significant to you in your present circumstances.

VERSE | WHAT TRUTH IT COMMUNICATES | HOW IT IMPACTS MY LIFE

If you were going away and knew that you would never see someone again, what would you say to him? Let's suppose you had led someone to Christ and had been used by God to disciple him along in his growth, and now you are leaving to move away. What would you say to him so that he would not fall away from God? This was the situation Paul found himself in with the Ephesian elders. Paul was on his way to Jerusalem. He knew he would never see these men again. He was fearful of the attacks from Satan, giving him the opportunity to destroy their lives. So what did he tell them on this final opportunity? That the key to their growth was going to be the Word of God. He also told them, in verse 32, that the Word of God would build them up and give them an inheritance. It would keep them strong and growing and enable them to stay the course. God's Word is the key to our spiritual lives. It must be the priority of each day. Does you life demonstrate the importance you claim for the Word of God? Do you organize your life in such a way that the Word of God is your priority every day? What needs to change to make it so?

SAY WHAT?
Observation: What do I see?

SO WHAT?
Interpretation: What does it mean?

NOW WHAT?
Application: How does it apply to me?

THEN WHAT?
Implementation: What do I do?

EXTRA READING
ACTS 20

ontrack devotions

#ontrackdevos

SAY WHAT?

What positive reasons might God have for wanting someone to go through hardships?

SO WHAT?

Why is it so hard for us to see the positives in hardship?

NOW WHAT?

How can you come to view hardships as Paul did?

THEN WHAT?

In light of this passage, what personal commitment can you make?

How could Paul, being led by the Spirit, conclude that God wanted him to go to Jerusalem, and others, also led by the Spirit, tell him not to go? One answer might be that they each had a different perspective on what the Spirit of God was telling them. Both were being told by the Spirit that Paul would face great hardships in Jerusalem. He would be imprisoned. To most people that would not be something to be desired, but avoided at all costs. After all, God would not want anyone to suffer, right? Paul was the greatest missionary in all of history. He was responsible for leading thousands to Christ and started churches all over the world. God could never want him in jail and destroy his ministry impacting the world. Right? Paul realized something that the elders forgot--God had a plan. They didn't consider that maybe God wanted Paul to go to Rome, at Rome's expense, to influence many leaders and prisoners for Christ. What awaited was not a bad situation to be avoided, but a painful experience that was exactly what God wanted for him. God's plan isn't always easy, but it is always best. Use today's questions to help you apply this truth to your own life.

EXTRA READING
ACTS 21

What happens to someone when he trusts Christ? Does he just get something added to who he already is? In other words, is he the same person who acquires a new part to his life? If you read today's section carefully, you realized that salvation means that you become a totally new person, not just some thing good added to the bad person you used to be. We see this truth demonstrated in Paul's testimony. He spoke to the crowd and reminded them of the kind of person he was before he trusted Christ. He was once a man who persecuted Christians, and, after salvation, he preached the same message he tried so hard to silence. He once hated Christ and everything about Him, but after salvation, became willing to die for Him. His conversion on the road to Damascus radically changed him. We often view salvation as a ticket to heaven. Our lives stay as they were before our salvation. If there isn't a change in your life, you have never been saved. The change may not be as drastic or as immediate as Paul's was, but it should still be there. Salvation means becoming a new person, not adding to the old one. How should you respond to what you see in your own life?

SAY WHAT?
Observation: What do I see?

SO WHAT?
Interpretation: What does it mean?

NOW WHAT?
Application: How does it apply to me?

THEN WHAT?
Implementation: What do I do?

EXTRA READING
ACTS 22

ontrack
devotions

#ontrackdevos

SAY WHAT?
What difficult circumstances are you now facing?

SO WHAT?
What could God's plan be for these circumstances?

NOW WHAT?
How should you respond to them?

THEN WHAT?
In light of this passage, what personal commitment can you make?

What do you think went through Paul's mind when the Lord came to him and spoke the words that we've just read in verse 11? Maybe he began to understand the plan of God for placing him prison. Paul had headed to Jerusalem knowing that persecution awaited him. He even had brothers in Christ tell him that he should not go because of the danger that awaited him. If you had been Paul, would you wonder why God had taken you from the mission field and put you into prison, away from those you were discipling? After the Lord's conversation, he began to understand. God was taking him to Rome, the economic and cultural capital of the world, to proclaim the message of Christ. On the way, God would give him the opportunity to share his story with hundreds of people who might not otherwise have heard the message of salvation. Paul must have been overwhelmed at the thought of God using such disastrous circumstances to accomplish His perfectly planned event. Are there circumstances in your life that make no sense? What could God's plan be? Why not commit today to trust God with every one of them?

EXTRA READING
ACTS 23

ontrackdevotions.com

Today, we find in this passage, one of the most common responses to the gospel and to Christianity in general. In fact, you may have already heard it when you shared the gospel. Did you notice it? It is found in verse 25. Paul had the opportunity to share the gospel with Felix. Felix, who was already familiar with the story of Christ, had spent time discussing the truth of God's Word with Paul. No doubt, there were occasions in which he seriously considered his own need to trust Christ as his Savior. On this occasion, however, Felix became afraid when he realized what Paul meant by what he said. He must have understood how lost he was. But, instead of responding by trusting Christ, he told Paul he would discuss it again later, "When I find it convenient." This response often has tragic consequences that are eternal. It makes me wonder if Felix ever found it "convenient." While this saddens us, it is also the attitude that many Christians have towards their walks with God. They have their devotions or reach out to the lost "When I find it convenient." Are you approaching God this way? Is it your priority, or something you do when it's convenient?

SAY WHAT?
Observation: What do I see?

SO WHAT?
Interpretation: What does it mean?

NOW WHAT?
Application: How does it apply to me?

THEN WHAT?
Implementation: What do I do?

EXTRA READING
ACTS 24

ontrack devotions

SAY WHAT?

Observation: What do I see?

SO WHAT?

Interpretation: What does it mean?

NOW WHAT?

Application: How does it apply to me?

THEN WHAT?

Implementation: What do I do?

Have you sat in church and heard from a missionary who needed money in order to be able to go to a foreign country to share his faith? In order to begin his ministry, he needed to raise money for his monthly support and for his expenses to get there. Imagine how helpful it would be if the government of the country he was going to paid all his expenses. How much would it require if his airfare and other travel expenses were paid for? Include in that his housing and food while he shared Christ with the lost. Sound impossible? This is exactly what happened to Paul. He went to Rome to share Christ, and Rome paid for it. They thought he was going to be tried and convicted for his ministry. His arrest resulted in Rome providing his transportation and meeting his physical needs all the way there. They assigned personal guards to Paul, who then had to listen to his message. What a miracle! How amazed Paul must have been to watch the plan of God unfold! This is an example to us of complete trust in God when all seems hopeless. God always has a plan! Do you believe that?

EXTRA READING
ACTS 25

The book of Proverbs was designed to help us in "attaining wisdom and discipline; in understanding words of insight; in acquiring a disciplined and prudent life, doing what is right and just and fair; in giving prudence to the simple, knowledge and discretion to the young." As you read through this chapter, write down the verses that are most significant to you in your present circumstances.

VERSE | WHAT TRUTH IT COMMUNICATES | HOW IT IMPACTS MY LIFE

SAY WHAT?

What was my life like before I met Christ? What would it have been like if I had not accepted Christ?

SO WHAT?

How did I come to trust Christ?

NOW WHAT?

How is my life different since or because I trusted Christ?

THEN WHAT?

What personal commitment should I make in light of this passage?

If you had an opportunity to share your faith with a group of people who do not know Jesus Christ, what would you say? How would you begin? What would you make sure to communicate? In today's reading, we receive an excellent example from the apostle Paul of how to share our faith with people who do not know Christ. God had again given Paul an opportunity that few men would have, to share with King Agrippa. Let's look closely at his example. He was polite and kind (26:2-3). Next, he shared with them what his life was like before he met Jesus Christ (26:4-11). He then shared with him how he had trusted Jesus Christ (26:12-18). He concluded by letting him know that his life had changed as a result of what God had done(26:19-23). This is an example we can all follow when we have the opportunity to share our faith with others. Use today's questions to put together your story so you can share it with others. If you need help, ask a spiritual leader in your life. Think of someone you can share it with when you are finished. Pray that God will give you an opportunity to share it. Then, look for the opportunities God will give you to share.

EXTRA READING
ACTS 26

When are people most open to the gospel? When do you have the greatest power to share Christ with others, either with words or by actions? The answer to both is in a crisis. In today's reading, we see Paul again taking advantage of a great moment of crisis to influence others with the message of Christ. The ship he was on was about to be destroyed. Paul took that opportunity to share with the crew that God would save them. He told them to eat food, but first made sure he gave thanks to God. For 14 days, they were in the midst of a great crisis. Paul did not panic or doubt God. He attempted to encourage the sailors to trust in the sovereignty of God, even though at the moment, it looked hopeless. As a result, all were saved, and the words of Paul proven true. What an incredible opportunity he must have had to share with these men once they arrived on shore. They must have been more open to the message after watching Paul's faith, knowing they were close to death themselves. We need to see crisis as an opportunity to demonstrate and share the message of Christ. Do you? Is someone open to your message today?

SAY WHAT?
Observation: What do I see?

SO WHAT?
Interpretation: What does it mean?

NOW WHAT?
Application: How does it apply to me?

THEN WHAT?
Implementation: What do I do?

EXTRA READING
ACTS 27

ontrack
devotions

#ontrackdevos

ANCHOR
CHRISTIAN UNIVERSITY

THIS HOPE WE HAVE AS AN ANCHOR OF THE SOUL, A HOPE BOTH SURE AND STEADFAST AND ONE WHICH ENTERS WITHIN THE VEIL, WHERE JESUS HAS ENTERED AS A FORERUNNER FOR US...

HEBREWS 6:19-20

AMPLIFYING THE MISSION OF THE LOCAL CHURCH WORLDWIDE THROUGH FAITH-INFUSED BIBLICAL TRAINING AND EDUCATION.

DEGREE PROGRAMS:

CHRISTIAN LEADERSHIP
CAMP MINISTRY
INTERCULTURAL MINISTRY

FAMILY MINISTRY
URBAN MINISTRY
YOUTH MINISTRY

ANCHORU.COM

Made in the USA
Middletown, DE
05 September 2019